Thank God for the life and ministry of Bill Bright and for this wonderful book. May it be a great blessing to you and encourage you to think supernaturally and do mighty things for the Lord.

From the Foreword by
JOHN C. MAXWELL

BILL BRIGHT'S
"THE JOY OF KNOWING GOD" SERIES

SUPERNATURAL
THINKING

DR. BILL BRIGHT

Victor®

The Bible Teacher's Teacher

COOK COMMUNICATIONS MINISTRIES
Colorado Springs, Colorado • Paris, Ontario
KINGSWAY COMMUNICATIONS LTD
Eastbourne, England

Victor® is an imprint of
Cook Communications Ministries,
Colorado Springs, CO 80918
Cook Communications, Paris, Ontario
Kingsway Communications, Eastbourne, England

THE JOY OF SUPERNATURAL THINKING
© 2005 by Bill Bright

First Printing, 2005
Printed in United States of America
1 2 3 4 5 6 7 8 9 10 Printing/Year 09 08 07 06 05

Cover Design: Brand Navigation, LLC

Library of Congress Cataloging-in-Publication Data

Bright, Bill.
  The joy of supernatural thinking : believing God for the impossible / Bill Bright.
    p. cm. -- (The joy of knowing God series ; bk. 6.)
  ISBN 0-7814-4253-2 (pbk.)
  1. Thought and thinking--Religious aspects--Christianity. 2. Christian life. 3.
Trust in God. 4. Belief and doubt. I. Title.
  BV4598.4.B75 2005
  248.4--dc22
                                        2004026884

Dedication

GLOBAL FOUNDING PARTNERS

The Bright Media Foundation continues the multi-faceted ministries of Bill and Vonette Bright for generations yet unborn. God has touched and inspired the Brights through the ministries of writers through the centuries. Likewise, they wish to pass along God's message in Jesus Christ as they have experienced it, seeking to inspire, train, and transform lives, thereby helping to fulfill the Great Commission each year until our Lord returns.

Many generous friends have prayed and sacrificed to support the Bright Media Foundation's culturally relevant, creative works, in print and electronic forms. The following persons specifically have helped to establish the foundation. These special friends will always be known as Global Founding Partners *of the Bright Media Foundation.*

Bill and Christie Heavener and family

Stuart and Debra Sue Irby and family

Edward E. Haddock Jr., Edye Murphy-Haddock, and the Haddock family

❖

To Dr. Joon Gon Kim, Dr. Bailey Marks, and Dr. Paul Eshleman—three beloved friends, dear colleagues, and supernatural thinkers whose hearts and minds God has used to help change the world.

Acknowledgments

It was my privilege to share fifty-four years, six months, and twenty days of married life with a man who loved Jesus passionately and served Him faithfully. Six months before his home going, Bill initiated what has become "The Joy of Knowing God" series. It was his desire to pass along to future generations the insights God had given him that they, too, could discover God's magnificence and live out the wonderful plan He has for their lives.

"The Joy of Knowing God" series is a collection of Bill Bright's top ten life-changing messages. Millions of people around the world have already benefited greatly from these spiritual truths and are now living the exciting Christian adventure that God desires for each of us.

On behalf of Bill, I want to thank the following team that helped research, compile, edit, and wordsmith the manuscripts and audio scripts in this series: Jim Bramlett, Rebecca Cotton, Eric Metaxas, Sheryl Moon, Cecil Price, Michael Richardson, Eric Stanford, and Rob Suggs.

I also want to thank Bill's longtime friends and Campus Crusade associates Bailey Marks and Ted Martin, who carefully reviewed the scripts and manuscripts for accuracy.

Bill was deeply grateful to Bob Angelotti and Don Stillman of Allegiant Marketing Group for their encouragement to produce this series and their ingenuity in facilitating distribution to so many.

A special thanks to Cook Communications and its team of dedicated professionals who partnered with Bright Media Foundation in this venture, as well as to Steve Laube, who brought us together.

Last but not least, I want to express my appreciation to Helmut Teichert, who worked faithfully and diligently in overseeing this team that Bill's vision would be realized, and to John Nill, CEO of Bright Media, who has helped me navigate the many challenges along this journey.

As a result of the hard work of so many, and especially our wonderful Lord's promise of His grace, I trust that multitudes worldwide will experience a greater joy by knowing God and His ways more fully.

With a grateful heart,
MRS. BILL BRIGHT (VONETTE)

Contents

Foreword

It is a great honor and privilege to be asked to provide this foreword for my dear friend Bill Bright, who, in July 2003, went to be with the Lord whom he served so long and so faithfully.

We miss Bill greatly but rejoice at his "graduation" and the fullness of joy he is experiencing in the glorious presence of our risen Lord and Savior Jesus Christ. We also joyfully press forward with the charge that both our Lord and Bill have given us—to boldly proclaim to the world God's great love and forgiveness available through Jesus Christ.

This book was one of the last projects Bill completed, surely appropriate because Bill was the epitome of supernatural thinking more than anyone I have ever known. The theme of this book was the driving principle of his life, and the contents summarize the main message he wants us to have as we, who are still in this world, continue to help fulfill the Great Commission to which he was so totally committed.

Bill Bright personified supernatural thinking for several reasons. First, he did not limit God in his thinking. He sometimes referred to the classic book *Your God Is Too Small* by renowned theologian and Bible translator J. B. Phillips. Phillips described how many people have a limited view of God: "If they could see beyond their little inadequate god, and glimpse the reality of God, they might even laugh a little and perhaps weep a little."

Bill could clearly see beyond such a "little inadequate god" and better than most people glimpsed "the reality of God."

This understanding and grasp of God's greatness shaped Bill's life and drove his accomplishments.

He also personified supernatural thinking in his exalted view of the Bible, which he often referred to as "God's holy, inspired, inerrant Word." The official Campus Crusade for Christ statement of faith, which Bill helped compose, says: "The sole basis of our beliefs is the Bible, God's infallible written Word ... We believe that it was uniquely, verbally and fully inspired by the Holy Spirit and that it was written without error (inerrant) in the original manuscripts." Bill's view was not blind acceptance of the Bible but instead was based on years of study and knowledge of biblical apologetics, plus God's revelation to his heart.

The third reason Bill embodied supernatural thinking was his tremendous faith—faith in God and faith in what God has said and promised in His Word. He knew God is totally reliable, without exception. He knew he could fully trust what God has promised. I strongly recommend Bill Bright's biography, *Amazing Faith* by Michael Richardson (WaterBrook Press, 2000). This testimony of a lifetime of dynamic faith will stir and inspire your heart and will give you greater insights into this great servant of God.

The Bible says, "With God everything is possible" (Matthew 19:26). While most people accept that intellectually, Bill Bright not only believed it in his heart, but also dared to live it daily. He continuously thought supernaturally, with God-inspired thoughts, with big thoughts, and he experienced big results for God's kingdom—results that many believe are more in a single lifetime than any other person in history. What God did during the life of this humble servant is absolutely astonishing.

Bill Bright was also gifted to be able to tell us how, in practical terms, to think supernaturally. His calling was to communicate God's wonderful truths in ways people can understand, which he has done again with this book. Hebrews 12:1 tells us, "We are surrounded by such a huge crowd of witnesses to the life of faith." Bill Bright is one of those witnesses. Let us learn from him—this giant of the faith—and serve the Lord with renewed perspective, commitment, and fervor.

Thank God for the life and ministry of Bill Bright and for this wonderful book. May it be a great blessing to you and encourage you to think supernaturally and do mighty things for the Lord.

—JOHN C. MAXWELL

―――――――― ❖ ――――――――

We can transcend natural possibilities and dwell
in the realm of the supernatural.

――――――――――――――

PART ONE

Thinking Supernaturally

"Everything is possible with God."

—Jesus Christ

1

The Greatest Adventure
of Your Life

I was scheduled to speak at a conference of Campus Crusade's key leaders—and I was unprepared. Normally, I would have searched the Scriptures and prepared my notes well ahead of such a speaking engagement, but this time there simply was no time available for preparation.

As I was literally on my way to the event, I searched my memory for a topic I had previously spoken on, one that might be appropriate for this meeting, but nothing came to mind. Finally, in desperation, I cried out to God for His help. It was then that something remarkable came to pass: I heard the gentle voice of God giving me the wisdom and guidance I needed.

God provided me not only with a topic but also with a sturdy and compelling outline. I knew this subject was precisely what the Lord desired for our leaders to hear. This is the outline God gave me that day:

You can live a supernatural life by:

thinking supernaturally,

praying supernaturally,

planning supernaturally,

loving supernaturally,

living supernaturally in the power of the Holy Spirit, and
expecting supernatural results.

It was no surprise to me that God blessed the words He
gave me. In all humility, I knew the Holy Spirit's message for
that group was literally rolling off my tongue. The response
was enthusiastic, and I have used the topic and outline on
many subsequent occasions with similar success.

The only question is whether we will seize the moment for the glory of God and boldly and aggressively reach out to the world with the gospel.

This book marks the first time my presentation on supernatural thinking has appeared in print. The wording and order of the outline have changed just a bit, but the concepts are the same ones God gave me on that special day years ago. His message of supernatural thinking is just as true now as it was then—and is perhaps even more relevant today than ever.

SUPERNATURAL THINKING

As I look about me, I see untold opportunities for furthering the Great Commission—Jesus' command to Christians to go into the world and share the good news of His love and forgiveness. Quantum advances in transportation and communication technologies give us every reason to envision millions of people coming to personal faith in our great Creator God and Savior. The only question is whether we will seize the moment for the glory of God and boldly and aggressively reach out to the world with the gospel. We need supernatural empowerment.

For many years, I have been interested in the frontiers that lie beyond mere human accomplishment. I have thought deeply about a mind-set focused not on what is naturally plausible but on what is supernaturally possible. This is how I began to use the term *supernatural thinking*.

I am persuaded there is no limit to what our almighty God can accomplish through us.

Of course, we have limits to what we can accomplish through unaided human strength and wisdom. But I am persuaded there is no limit to what our almighty God can accomplish through us. His Word, the Bible, tells us this truth over and over. Consider these examples:

- Speaking to His disciples about how sinful people might be saved, Jesus said, "Humanly speaking, it is impossible. But not with God. Everything is possible with God" (Mark 10:27).
- On another occasion, the father of a troubled child asked Jesus to do something if He could. Jesus responded, "What do you mean, 'If I can'? ... Anything is possible if a person believes" (Mark 9:23).
- The apostle Paul, referring to living a fulfilled life under any material circumstances, wrote, "I can do everything with the help of Christ who gives me the strength I need" (Philippians 4:13).

Empowered by God, we can go beyond paltry human potential. We can transcend natural possibilities and dwell in the realm of the supernatural. We can live the glorious life of believing God for the impossible. And we can do all this by learning to think supernaturally, then trusting God for what He wants to do through us.

At this point, let me be clear that supernatural thinking, as I experience it, has nothing to do with practicing magic, manipulating natural forces, or cooperating with demons, spirits, or mediums. Rather, this kind of thinking is supernatural because God infuses the mind and heart with thoughts, ideas, and plans that transcend normal human thinking. It is, in short, thinking the thoughts that the God of the Bible chooses to give us for the advancement of His plans in the world.

Supernatural thinking has been the basis of my nearly sixty years of ministry. Everything I have done, I have done in response to the Bible's promise: "God is working in you, giving you the desire to obey him and the power to do what pleases him" (Philippians 2:13). In other words, whatever God tells us to do, He will enable us to do.

In the following chapters I will relate stories from my own life and from the lives of others who have discovered the power of supernatural thinking. As you read these stories, the prayer of my heart is that you will desire to experience the creative energy that is available through the power of the Holy Spirit, lifting you into bold acts of faith in sharing the magnificent life we have in Jesus Christ.

You can begin to live supernaturally if you love God, obey His commands, and trust His promises. Let this book move you in that direction. Then, when you come to embrace the lifestyle of supernatural thinking, the greatest adventure of your life will begin.

2

The Case for Different Thinking

The philosopher Ralph Waldo Emerson, reflecting on the way new ideas shake up the status quo, once said, "Beware when the great God lets loose a thinker on this planet." Those words are never truer than when the thinker is a man or woman who thinks not just excellent, self-generated thoughts but truly *supernatural* thoughts—ones sent from God—and then acts on them. That is how the world is changed.

Today, the thoughts that seem to have the greatest currency are selfish, petty, and even cruel. Even among followers of Christ, far too many think thoughts and dream dreams that are ordinary, uninspired, and downright timid. Where are the saints who envision themselves doing great deeds for God? Where are the ones who can see kingdom opportunities in places where others only see obstacles? Why don't we plot a course of action that requires God to empower us to complete it—and that will bring great glory to Him when it succeeds?

My friends, it is time for a revolution of godly thoughts and great plans. We must leave mediocrity behind, vacating the premises where the common strain of thinking resides. What we need today are thoughts capable of enflaming hearts, challenging God's servants to action, and drawing many into a love relationship with the Lord. For us, there should be no small ambitions, no puny expectations.

❖

For us, there should be no small ambitions, no puny expectations.

Listen to this assurance from our Lord Jesus Christ: "Anyone who believes in me will do the same works I have done, and even greater works, because I am going to be with the Father." Think for a moment about the amazing things Jesus accomplished while on earth. He says we can do even greater works than these because, after ascending to heaven, He sent the Holy Spirit to empower us. That is why Jesus could offer this shocking promise: "Ask anything in my name, and I will do it!" (John 14:12, 14).

To ask for God to empower us in a daring form of service to Him, we first must be able to imagine such service. That is, we first must *think* it. And the way we think really matters. Scripture tells us, "As [a man] thinks in his heart, so is he" (Proverbs 23:7 NKJV). As Christian believers, our thinking has been changed. Scripture assures us, "We have the mind of Christ" (1 Corinthians 2:16). And thus our thinking—and our lives—can be made to conform to God's ways as we cooperate with Him. Romans 12 instructs, "Let God transform you into a new person by changing the way you think" (verse 2).

Many of us have not yet been fully transformed through a change in our thinking. But as believers, we *can* be so transformed, because we have the Holy Spirit. And that is why I want to urge upon you and upon all Christians what I like to call *supernatural thinking*. Supernatural thinking is imagining, planning, and doing things for God that would be impossible to accomplish by mere human effort. The vision comes *from* God, the service is *for* God, and the work can be done only *by* God through us.

THE PURPOSE OF SUPERNATURAL THINKING

Many people speak of "thinking big" or about "reaching their full potential." In the right contexts, these may be worthy objectives. But I want to make clear that supernatural thinking is something else entirely, for its object is very different.

Supernatural thinking is not about getting ahead in business. It is not about doing things that give us pleasure or make our lives more comfortable. It is not for any worldly accomplishments. Rather, it is for serving God in the ways He chooses. And that means ministry.

All of our supernatural plans should be built around the Great Commission to make disciples of the nations.

> Jesus came and told his disciples, "I have been given
> complete authority in heaven and on earth. Therefore, go
> and make disciples of all the nations, baptizing them in the
> name of the Father and the Son and the Holy Spirit. Teach
> these new disciples to obey all the commands I have given
> you. And be sure of this: I am with you always, even to the
> end of the age."
>
> MATTHEW 28:18–20

I believe God expects every Christian to be a "world Christian." When our Lord and Savior Jesus Christ spoke the

Great Commission, He was not speaking to a small number of His followers; He called every single one of us, and He specified the entire globe.

For decades now, I have tested every thought and plan by how it can help fulfill Christ's Great Commission. At first I was hoping to lead hundreds of people to Christ—that seemed like a big goal at the time. Then I desired to see thousands come to the Lord. Then millions. Now, in the sunset of my life, I have on my heart the billions in the world who do not yet know our wonderful Lord.

I am by no means discouraged. How could I be when I serve a Savior who has declared that the gates of hell will not prevail against His church? But while I am not discouraged, I am restless. Jesus gave us the Great Commission two thousand years ago, yet we still have so far to go in taking His message of love to people who need it. Every day people are dying without hearing about Jesus Christ, and that is the greatest tragedy imaginable.

If the Great Commission is to be fulfilled, it will take supernatural thinking.

If the Great Commission is to be fulfilled, it will take supernatural thinking. That is, it will take thinking of a whole different order from that to which we have grown accustomed.

CHARACTERISTICS OF SUPERNATURAL THINKING

Supernatural thinking is God thinking through a yielded human mind. This thinking flows through a bold believer in the God of the universe and of Calvary and of the empty tomb. For today's marketplace of ideas, it might be called "God-Think." Supernatural thinking is obeying the command to "have the mind of Christ" (1 Corinthians 2:16).

As we consider this type of thinking, certain characteristics stand out.

- Supernatural thinking requires total dependence on the God of the Bible. "It is impossible to please God without faith" (Hebrews 11:6).
- Supernatural thinking exalts the Lord Jesus Christ. "God raised him up to the heights of heaven and gave him a name that is above every other name, so that at the name of Jesus every knee will bow, in heaven and on earth and under the earth, and every tongue will confess that Jesus Christ is Lord, to the glory of God the Father" (Philippians 2:9–11).

> *Supernatural thinking is God thinking through a yielded human mind.*

- Supernatural thinking furthers the sharing of the good news. Jesus said, "When the Holy Spirit has come upon you, you will receive power and will tell people about me everywhere" (Acts 1:8).
- Supernatural thinking requires the working of the Holy Spirit in ways and times beyond our imagining. "It is not by force nor by strength, but by my Spirit, says the LORD Almighty" (Zechariah 4:6).
- Supernatural thinking is opposed by the faithless. "The people of the world will hate you because you belong to me," Christ said, "for they don't know God who sent me" (John 15:21).
- Supernatural thinking is accompanied by passion and devotion. "One thing I do, forgetting those things which are behind and reaching forward to those things which are

ahead, I press toward the goal for the prize of the upward call of God in Christ Jesus" (Philippians 3:13–14 NKJV).

- Supernatural thinking arises from a lifestyle of prayer, fasting, and meditation. "Study this Book of the Law continually. Meditate on it day and night so you may be sure to obey all that is written in it. Only then will you succeed" (Joshua 1:8).

Does the description of this kind of thinking inspire you? Perhaps you are intrigued but are not sure whether supernatural thinking is for you. I have a sobering truth for you: You are not capable of supernatural thinking. Neither am I. None of us is capable of it on our own, yet any of us can experience supernatural thinking and use it *as we receive it from God through faith.*

Supernatural thinking is altogether possible for any person who is yielded to God in mind and heart. He does extraordinary things through ordinary persons. If we need encouragement that supernatural thinking is a possibility for us, we need only look to the supernatural thinkers who have gone before us.

A ROLL CALL OF SUPERNATURAL THINKERS

I cast my mind back over many people I have known who displayed supernatural thinking.

For instance, my thoughts turn to a man who felt a great personal burden for the children orphaned by the Korean conflict of the 1950s. Through God's power, Bob Pierce moved people all over America to care for the children of their wartime enemies. His ministry (as often happens) broke loose, transcending its original vision. In the decades that have followed the Korean conflict, whenever and wherever disaster occurred, World Vision has been there to offer relief and assistance. Bob Pierce was a supernatural thinker.

Then I think of a young man who sold his car to help finance a tiny restaurant called the Dwarf Grill. In time that little restaurant became a worldwide food chain—one famous for remaining closed on Sundays to honor God's commandment of rest (Exodus 20:8). The man's name is Truett Cathy, and he, too, is a supernatural thinker. He has built his company on solid biblical values. He helps his youthful employees with scholarships for college. He operates camps and programs for young people. His franchise, Chick-fil-A, may sell chicken sandwiches, but with their children's meals, they also give away materials that promote moral values.

I also recall a college football coach named Bill McCartney. Many thought he should stay in the field he knew so well. But God gave him a vision for helping other men serve and worship God. The movement he started—Promise Keepers—within a few years was bringing together thousands of men in stadiums to discuss loving Jesus, being responsible husbands and fathers, and breaking down barriers between ethnic groups. In a nation where women typically are the backbone of churches, McCartney's ministry has touched the lives of countless men, leading to healing for their families and making our country a better place.

My thoughts turn to a California orange grower who taught a Sunday school class. His class became so popular that it had to move into the local city hall to accommodate everyone who wanted to hear his biblical lessons. When radio came along (this was the 1920s), this godly man thought supernaturally about the new medium. He recognized what could be done for God's kingdom and organized a radio ministry—cutting-edge thinking for that era. His ministry bore fruit, and Charles E. Fuller continued to train young men for ministry. This led to the seminary that bears his name today. I was a student there during its first years, and I knew Dr. Fuller personally and have seen the worldwide results of his supernatural thinking.

Then I think of a woman of God who once said, "There is no magic in small plans. When I consider my ministry, I think of the world. Anything less than that would not be worthy of Christ nor of His will for my life." Our amazing Lord used her to change the face of Christian education all across the world through her books and teaching curriculum, through her conference center, and through her personal work with thousands of young men, including Billy Graham, Richard Halverson, Robert Munger, and me. Henrietta C. Mears said that she "dreamed big," but I call it thinking supernaturally.

I could name many other supernatural thinkers, including D. James Kennedy, Pat Robertson, Bob Reccord, Steve Douglass, Oral Roberts, Adrian Rogers, Thomas Trask, Charles Stanley, Paul Crouch, Dawson Trotman, Torrey Johnson, and so many more.[1]

Someday the list of supernatural thinkers could include *your* name. There is no reason in heaven or on earth why you cannot walk with those giants. The power, the vision, and the opportunity all come from God; you need only provide the obedience and the faith for supernatural thinking.

A CHALLENGE

Throughout my ministry, I have assured people that God has a wonderful plan for their lives. A part of that wonderful plan includes cooperating with the Lord as He brings people into His kingdom. In other words, it includes being a supernatural thinker in the special ways that God has prepared for me and for you.

When was the last time you believed God for something the world considers impossible? I believe most Christians never do so, and yet what greater demonstration could be made of faith in our wonderful Lord and Savior, who possesses all authority in heaven and earth? How else may we come to know and believe just how unlimited is the power of His hand on our behalf?

> *When was the last time you believed God for something the world considers impossible?*

Begin ridding your mind of the world's misperceptions about what is or is not possible. Every day of your life, remind yourself there are no limits to what God can do and wants to do through you. There are no boundaries or limitations to what He can do through you if you are willing to obediently surrender to His sovereign will and His Holy Spirit.

Do not be content with ordinary effectiveness. Do not settle for second—or third—best. Do not confine yourself to goals that offer a ready model or that seem easy to accomplish. Do not think too little of yourself, given that God is acting through you. He has chosen you and commissioned you. And He promises to work in and through you as He calls you to join Him in His glorious work. And while He remains without doubt the powerful partner in this work, the part He gives you to do is strategic.

I am not saying being a supernatural thinker is easy. In fact, the more we live and work in the Holy Spirit, the more tests and trials come into our lives. Our adversary, the Evil One, becomes concerned and mounts a counterattack. And it makes sense that he directs his efforts in directions where he is losing ground.

But we can be assured that our loving and gracious Lord will guide us safely through each trial (1 Corinthians 10:13).

Never let your frustration over details or setbacks deter you from continuing to pursue the great goal God has set out for you. And never doubt your God-given dream, given to you on the mountaintop, as you walk through the valley of testing. Keep on believing! Your faith and patience will be rewarded when God reveals His way in His time.

As children, we read fairy tales in which the characters brave dangers in a forest to live "happily ever after." As we have grown older, we have learned to enjoy novels and movies that depict people doing exciting things we might wish to do. But be certain of this: The story God is writing in history, with flesh-and-blood characters and an ending that is out of this world, is grander and more exciting than any other could ever be. It has all the thrills, comradeship, surprises, risks, harrowing escapes, sense of accomplishment, and pride of being on the winning side that we could ever ask for. And best of all, it is *real*.

You can be a part of this story, and as no minor character. A chapter has been written for you. Do not miss it! Be a supernatural thinker!

---

1. Dr. Billy Graham became an international evangelist. Dr. Richard Halverson became chaplain of the United States Senate. Dr. Robert Munger became a pastor and author of the popular book *My Heart—Christ's Home*. Dr. D. James Kennedy is the pastor of Coral Ridge Presbyterian Church in Fort Lauderdale, Florida. Dr. Pat Robertson is founder of the Christian Broadcasting Network. Bob Reccord is president of the North American Mission Board. Dr. Steve Douglass is the president of Campus Crusade for Christ International. Dr. Oral Roberts is the founder of the university that bears his name. Dr. Adrian Rogers served three times as president of the Southern Baptist Convention. Dr. Thomas Trask is general superintendent of the Assemblies of God. Dr. Charles Stanley is the pastor of the First Baptist Church of Atlanta, Georgia, and a popular speaker. Paul Crouch is the founder of the Trinity Broadcasting Network. Dawson Trotman was the founder of The Navigators ministry. Dr. Torrey Johnson was a pastor and president of Youth for Christ.

3

Thinking That Goes Above and Beyond

Some decades ago Dr. Norman Vincent Peale proposed the concept of "positive thinking." His idea was that, through a positive belief in God and ourselves, we could achieve greater things. Later, Dr. Robert Schuller began advancing his conception of "possibility thinking." He urged people not to focus on obstacles and problems but rather to consider what might be accomplished. Both Christian men have made valuable contributions with their ideas. But I believe supernatural thinking goes beyond either positive thinking or possibility thinking, for supernatural thinking is nothing less than thinking thoughts that God gives us.

Positive thinking says, "I will not let my problems discourage or paralyze me." Possibility thinking says, "I will explore ways to defeat my problems." Supernatural thinking says, "I will seek God for how He wants to raise me above the ordinary and do something new through me that I could never do on my own." Supernatural thinking represents an entirely new perspective, one that sees the impossible as possible through God's involvement. As Jesus said, "What is impossible from a human perspective is possible with God" (Luke 18:27).

The letter to the Ephesians calls God "Him who is able to do exceedingly abundantly above all that we ask or think, according to the power that works in us" (3:20 NKJV). His works go beyond our natural ability to comprehend them. If we are to grasp them, we must use supernatural thinking—thinking that transcends and transforms the natural.

GOING ABOVE AND BEYOND

As commonplace as airplane travel has become, if we stop to think about it, we have to admit it is a remarkable thing. In airplanes we can fly across the country or around the world in a matter of just hours. That is amazing!

But there is an even more remarkable kind of travel— space travel. While an airplane remains in the earth's atmosphere, a space shuttle can circle the entire earth in just ninety minutes or so. That is *really* amazing!

Natural thinking is like airplane travel according to the laws of aerodynamics, while supernatural thinking is like space travel according to the laws of astrophysics. Natural thinking can accomplish a great deal; supernatural thinking lifts us to an entirely greater dimension. It is thinking God's thoughts after Him.

The Lord tells us, "My thoughts are completely different from yours.... And my ways are far beyond anything you could imagine. For just as the heavens are higher than the earth, so are my ways higher than your ways and my thoughts higher than your thoughts" (Isaiah 55:8–9). In supernatural thinking, we are lifted above the normal level of human thoughts and are given access to something of God's higher thoughts.

Of course, God does not share all His thoughts with us. But He does share with us those that relate to our part in His plans for the world; He shares key points of His will for our lives.

I have asked God for the supernatural dimension of thinking virtually every day since I received Christ as my personal Savior. Upon waking, I thank God for the day and for the opportunity of trusting and obeying and praising Him. I then ask specifically, "Lord, think with my mind, love with my heart, speak with my lips, wear me as a suit of clothes." And I believe and know from experience that He answers this prayer, because it is consistent with His commands and promises.

Time and again, I have been able to press on, often against the naysaying of others around me, because I had received my goals from a supernatural Person. When I was convinced God wanted to accomplish some new, ambitious work through me, I continued to believe God even as I heard people cry, "That's impossible! Don't bother asking God for that—it can't be done." As I looked to God, the sole object of my faith, I claimed His promises. Many others have done the same, including my good friend Dr. Joon Gon Kim.

ABOVE AND BEYOND IN SOUTH KOREA

In the summer of 1972, Dr. Kim, the South Korean director of Campus Crusade for Christ International, stood on the platform at EXPLO '72. Held in Dallas, Texas, this event brought together approximately eighty-five thousand people for a week of discipleship and evangelism training. At the conclusion of EXPLO '72, Dr. Kim announced to the Campus Crusade leadership that he believed at least three hundred thousand people would gather for training in his native South Korea two years later.

To those who understood logistical realities—to "natural" thinkers, in other words—a South Korean EXPLO was surely an impossible dream. Were there really 300,000 South Koreans interested in attending such an event? If so, how could we feed, lodge, and care for so many? Would government authorities cooperate with Christian planners? Where would the money for the event come from?

This would be one of the boldest, most ambitious undertakings in the history of Christianity, and Dr. Kim knew he was skirting disaster and risking embarrassment. But God had told him to undertake this ambitious, unprecedented event. He was a man with a mind fixed on eternity and eternity's God; his was a supernatural mind-set. His outlook was the product not of spreadsheets but of fervent, dependent prayer, and he was convinced that he was following the will of God.

> *His outlook was the product not of spreadsheets but of fervent, dependent prayer.*

When Dr. Kim presented his dream for EXPLO '74 to his fellow staff members, nearly every one of them was opposed to the idea. The project, they thought, was too large. No assembly on that scale had ever been brought together in recorded history. Dr. Kim was planning an event nearly four times as large as EXPLO '72. At a planning session the doubtful staff members went to the blackboard and wrote out *seventy-five* reasons why Dr. Kim's plans should *not* be undertaken.

Dr. Kim allowed each of them to have his or her say, and then he calmly explained that God had told him what to do. As Dr. Kim's plan, yes, it would be outrageous. But as God's plan, it could not fail. Because it was God's will, EXPLO '74 needed to be pursued with supernatural faith. Dr. Kim addressed each of their concerns. Then, he encouraged each of his workers to walk in faith, joining him in believing God for the supernatural. Most of his staff members took his advice, and they helped make history—the largest gathering of Christians in training ever.

God brought matters together in a way the world had never seen. There were all-night prayer vigils involving hundreds of thousands of Koreans. Huge pressure cookers, capable of cooking five thousand meals at a time, were invented just in time for EXPLO '74. The government cooperated. The members of twelve thousand Korean churches rolled up their collective sleeves and handled every detail and every challenge under the guidance of the visionary Dr. Kim.

Many details could have gone awry, but instead the results were wonderful and glorious, both planned and unplanned. In the end, there were 323,419 delegates who attended the six-day conference. One of the Seoul daily newspapers reported that more than 1.5 million people attended the largest evening session of EXPLO '74. Gospel presentations and teachings were conducted in four languages, and over a million people indicated salvation decisions when I gave an invitation to receive Christ.

At the beginning of 1974, less than one in five South Koreans professed to be a Christian. By the end of the century, the number of professed Christians was near 50 percent. EXPLO '74 had started a national tidal wave of salvation and revival, and all of it happened because of the supernatural thinking of one man who resolved to saturate his country with the gospel and fill the kingdom of heaven with South Koreans.

Can one person achieve such an impossible goal? From a human perspective, the answer is certainly no. But God never desires that we do anything from a human perspective. After all, we have the mind of Christ.

THE MIND OF CHRIST

One of the most astounding proclamations in Scripture (and one we largely ignore) is the biblical promise that we have the mind of Christ. In his first letter to the church at Corinth, Paul wrote, "We can understand these things, for we have the mind of Christ" (2:16).

Consider what this means. We are prone to shrink back in fear, for it seems almost blasphemous to speak of carrying,

> ❖
>
> *God desires us to boldly attempt great things for Him.*

in our fallen and imperfect selves, the mind of the One who is the Alpha and the Omega, whose hands formed this universe, who raised others from the dead and defeated death on the cross. It is Christ whom we worship; how can we possibly speak of possessing His mind?

Surely we are humbled and even staggered by such seemingly preposterous words. But Scripture speaks them, and we can claim them with confidence. God desires us to boldly attempt great things for Him. The church is, in a supernatural sense, the living body of Christ, and so we carry on His works, miracles and all. We are to do all that He did—and more and greater. And it begins with thinking as He thinks.

How, then, do we think with the mind of Christ? How can we become supernatural thinkers? This occurs in two ways: by transformation and by imitation. The first is a gift we accept; the second is an action we initiate.

The key passage about the transforming of our minds is found at Romans 12:2: "Don't copy the behavior and customs of this world, but let God transform you into a new person by changing the way you think. Then you will know what God wants you to do, and you will know how good and pleasing and perfect his will really is."

The key words are "let God transform you into a new person by changing the way you think." God changes us from the inside out, beginning with our thinking. Not only do we then know His will, but also we are pleased by it and motivated to perform it. We need only cooperate in inviting Him to do His great work.

The Holy Spirit labors constantly within us to bring this about. Second Corinthians 3:18 tells us, "As the Spirit of the Lord works within us, we become more and more like him and reflect his glory even more."

But taking on the mind of Christ is more than merely a passive acceptance of the work God wants done. We must *embrace* the transformation, and we must ask to possess more and more of that mind-set every day, until there is nothing in life we do not see from the perspective of God's supernatural thinking.

Peter wrote, "Since Christ suffered for us in the flesh, arm yourselves also with the same mind" (1 Peter 4:1 NKJV). With the idea of "arming" ourselves, Peter drew on military terminology. A soldier who fails to take up arms will fall in battle. In the battle of life, we arm ourselves with the mind of Christ, striving to know Him through His Word and through abiding with Him in prayer.

The closer we come to knowing His mind, the more we dwell in His loving presence. The deeper He comes to dominate our thoughts, the more like Him we become. We see the world as He sees it, and we feel the emotions He feels as we look upon this hurting world. We feel the confidence of knowing His overcoming power. We feel the hope and joy of knowing that He is truly the Lord of all. And we face our own trials with courage and resolve, as Christ Himself faced the cross.

Therefore, we see that our minds are molded "from both ends." The Spirit does His ongoing work of transforming us into Christ's image, and the Spirit enables us to do our part by seeking in His power to become more and more like Him.

Does this sound like something you would like? When was the last time you consciously opened your mind to God, inviting Him to pour in any vision for ministry that He wished, no matter how difficult or extraordinary it might seem? Are you prepared to go to people who are spiritually needy and love them with the love of God, even when they are not lovable?

Supernatural thinking is not just for the favored few, the so-called giants of the faith. All Christians can do great things if they will trust God and allow themselves to think His supernatural thoughts. The work that results from your supernatural thinking may not be as spectacular or as public as EXPLO '74. But it will have a powerful impact for the kingdom in its own way, fulfilling God's will for you and bringing Him delight as you are faithful to His calling.

The work of supernatural thinking and doing is God's, but if you desire to be used by God in this way, you can start the process by making yourself ready and available to Him.

4

The Process of Supernatural Thinking

I believe we live in an age when miracles can still happen, but too often we do not expect the miraculous or the impossible. Supernatural thinking looks at life from a faith perspective that considers all things possible with God. Think of it: How glorious it would be to the praise of our Lord Jesus if we chose a lifestyle of supernatural thinking—and lived this way every day!

Is there anything we can do to prepare to receive a supernatural vision, burden, or dream? How do we respond once we have received that vision?

I would like to share with you the process of supernatural thinking as I have experienced it over the past six decades. It has five stages: knowing God, surrendering to God, seeking a vision from God, abandoning self-effort, and adopting a supernatural perspective.

Stage 1: Knowing God

This may sound elementary, but it is a fact that supernatural thinking is reserved for people who have a supernatural dimension to their lives. We cannot expect supernatural thinking without Christ in our lives. This truth cannot be bartered or bargained or begged. It can only be believed by simple, childlike trust in Jesus of Nazareth, the Son of God and Savior of the world. It is all about knowing God personally.

I became a follower of Christ as a young adult after moving to California to begin a business. I thought I was self-sufficient and had everything I needed. But when some believers introduced me to Christ and helped me get the teaching I needed, I realized I was incomplete without the Lord. I asked Him into my heart, and from that moment my life was changed forever.

At that time I also was filled with a hunger to know God better—a hunger that has never since been fully satisfied. And that is how it should work for all of us. We not only need to *know* God, in a personal sense, but also need to *know about* God more every day. As Paul testified, "Everything else is worthless when compared with the priceless gain of knowing Christ Jesus my Lord" (Philippians 3:8).

Once we become Christians, we begin a lifelong process of understanding God better through our individual experience of Him. As we get to know Him better, we see that He is worthy of our trust to do the amazing through us.

> *Learning more about our wonderful God is an endless and delightful exercise.*

Learning more about our wonderful God is an endless and delightful exercise.

We are privileged to cultivate our relationship with God through what are known as the spiritual disciplines. These include praying, reading Scripture, meditating on Scripture, worshiping, and much more. A supernatural thinker practices spiritual disciplines daily.

Knowing God and determining to learn more about Him all the time are great starting points. But then we have to move on to surrendering our will and our life fully to Him.

STAGE 2: SURRENDERING TO GOD

God is the King; we are His subjects. He is our Master; we are His slaves. We need to submit to God in all things so that we may serve Him in the ways He chooses. In part, this means clearing away obstacles to God's work by putting away the sin in our lives.

> *We need to submit to God in all things so that we may serve Him in the ways He chooses.*

God does not require that any of us be perfect in order to serve Him. (If He waited for us to be perfect, we would never get around to serving Him in this life!) We are all tempted, and we all sometimes give in to that temptation. But people who are dedicated to rooting out the sin in their life and pursuing holiness are people who please our Holy God.

For years, I have advocated a practice I call "Spiritual Breathing." Spiritual Breathing is "exhaling" the impure through confession of sin, then "inhaling" the pure through receiving a new filling of the Holy Spirit. In other words, as soon as you realize that you have done wrong, you deal with it immediately by going to God for His mercy. We have God's command: "Let the Holy Spirit fill and control you" (Ephesians 5:18). And we have God's promise: "If we confess our sins to him, he is faithful and just to forgive us and to cleanse us from every wrong" (1 John 1:9). On the basis of God's own words to us, I advise you to practice Spiritual Breathing if you desire to think supernaturally.

In addition to clearing away sin's obstacles to the work of God, surrendering also means committing ourselves to doing whatever God asks of us and living for Him alone. We can all get involved with our worldly concerns and our selfish desires to the point that we forget about living for God. But becoming a Christian does not mean that God has become an add-on to an already busy life. Rather, as I have said, He is the King. He owns our lives. We are to turn control over to Him entirely, so that His will for our lives becomes our will for our lives.

The reality of this complete commitment became a landmark in my life and that of my wife. During our early married years, my beloved Vonette and I realized that we had different ideas about how we would live our lives, and it brought us into conflict. Were we most concerned about our family? Did we value prosperity and material possessions highest? What were we going to live for?

After thinking and talking at length, we made a decision. We realized that, above all else, we had to live for the service of God. Everything else would fall into its proper place if we did that. So we wrote contracts in which we pledged to be slaves of Jesus for the rest of our days, and then we signed them. That is how we surrendered to Him.

God honored our commitment. Do you know how I know that? Within twenty-four hours of signing the contract, I received a vision from Him for what would eventually become Campus Crusade for Christ.

STAGE 3: SEEKING A VISION FROM GOD

The day after signing the contract with Vonette, I was going about my normal business when God suddenly and unexpectedly spoke to me. Out of the blue, He made it clear that

He wanted me to help fulfill the Great Commission during my generation, and He wanted me to do it initially through ministry to college students.

That was my vision, and that was the way in which I received it. Your vision from God may look quite different. Your vision may come in the form of a burden you feel for some particular need, such as relieving the misery of the homeless. Or the vision may come in the form of a specific dream, such as showing love to members of a religious cult in the hope of bringing them to the truth. The service to which God calls you may be the sort that gets lots of attention, or it may involve behind-the-scenes work.

This vision might be almost anything, but it will not be small; it will be big, daring, risky. It will be high-impact work in its own special way. And it will contribute to God's primary goals of evangelism and disciple-building as embodied in the Great Commission.

Our God is big. And the human race He has created is beautifully diverse. Is it any wonder, then, that God has many different kinds of supernatural thinking in store for His people? After all, this is the God who declares, "Behold, I will do a new thing" (Isaiah 43:19 NKJV). Expect to be surprised.

The diversity in the types of supernatural thinking relates to the diversity of spiritual gifts that God has distributed among Christ's body (1 Corinthians 12). Our spiritual gifts are the resources God has planted within us to enable us to do what He calls us to. We can expect the vision God gives us to match the spiritual gifts with which He equips

This vision might be almost anything, but it will not be small; it will be big, daring, risky.

us. The same God has planned both the call and the resources from eternity past.

One more point: God gives big dreams of service to people who have already proved themselves faithful to Him in smaller ways.

In a parable about three servants who were entrusted with their master's wealth, how did Jesus say the master rewarded the two faithful servants? By giving them a week's vacation at a popular Dead Sea spa? No! By giving them greater responsibility. The master said to each of them, "Well done, my good and faithful servant. You have been faithful in handling this small amount, so now I will give you many more responsibilities. Let's celebrate together!" (Matthew 25:21).

I had spent several years of service to our Lord in the Hollywood Presbyterian Church as a layman active in visitation, as a deacon in leadership, and in studies at two seminaries. I have received not only my original vision for campus ministry, but also many other visions over the years for bigger and bigger service. You, too, may receive a big vision for service today—and an even bigger vision later on.

Whether your history of service to God is long or short, start now to be faithful in what God has already given you. And in the meantime, seek Him prayerfully for greater things. Be prepared: The glorious vision of service He may give you will be thrilling. And when He gives it, expect also to be overwhelmed by it to the point that you realize your own resources are far too insignificant to get you there.

STAGE 4: ABANDONING SELF-EFFORT

The vision that God gives us is, by definition, too great for us to accomplish in our own abilities. Test a suspected supernatural vision by asking whether you can fulfill it without God. Our resources are simply not adequate, because if the vision is God-sized, it will take God's resources to make it a reality.

When God gave me the vision for starting Campus Crusade, I may have had some ideas at the outset

The glorious vision of service He may give you will be thrilling.

about my own abilities enabling me to serve God in this new endeavor. But I quickly realized that the vision went far beyond my puny abilities. The vision could not be realized in any natural sense. And so it has turned out to be far above what I could ask or even think (see Ephesians 3:20). So it will turn out for you, too, with the vision that God gives you.

We are like Gideon, an unconventional general in Israel's early history. God pared Gideon's military forces down from thousands to just three hundred warriors so that when God gave Israel the victory against the hordes of Midian, all would know that He had done it (Judges 7). Likewise, God has given us limited resources so that we will always turn to Him for help and give Him the glory.

All this means that our attitude toward our work for God should begin and end with humility. Jesus said that the greatest in the kingdom of heaven are those who are as humble as a little child (Matthew 18:4). Who does God favor? Those who think highly of themselves and let others know it? Those who amass power for themselves and use that power selfishly? Not so. "God ... shows favor to the humble" (James 4:6).

And this is why godly leadership looks much different from its worldly counterpart. In God's kingdom, leaders are servants, not "lords" (see Matthew 20:25–28). Therefore, as you go about fulfilling the vision God has given you, abandon any idea that there is something great in you. What is great is *what God is doing through you*. It is all about God.

We do not say, "I can do all things." We say, "I can do all things through Christ who strengthens me" (Philippians 4:13 NKJV).

STAGE 5: ADOPTING A SUPERNATURAL PERSPECTIVE

Jesus could have been speaking about the supernatural dream that God wants to give you when He said, "Humanly speaking, it is impossible. But not with God. Everything is possible with God" (Mark 10:27).

When we realize we are incapable of accomplishing the goal God has given us, we do not despair. Instead, we turn to Him and rely on His power to not only direct but also enable our service. The filament in a lightbulb does not shine because it tries hard; rather, it shines because it is connected to a power source. We are the same way—we are successful only as we serve as a conduit for God's power in the world.

When I received the vision for Campus Crusade, few people even wanted to *talk* about fulfilling the Great Commission. Technologies that would enable a worldwide ministry of the sort I had in mind did not exist at that time. There were no commercial jet planes, no satellites, no computers, no cell phones, no Internet. I realized that I had to trust God to provide the means for fulfilling the vision He had given me. My part was just to get going on college campuses. Our slogan was "Win the campus today; win the world tomorrow."

This mind-set is needed all the way through. We must

persevere not just in our labors, but also in our faith. "He who has begun a good work in you will complete it" (Philippians 1:6 NKJV). As we persevere through obstacles and see God overcome them through His power, we will learn that it is all of God, every bit of it.

GO BOLDLY

We can learn great lessons about supernatural thinking from the Israelites' conquest of Canaan. This was the Promised Land, the homeland of their dreams. The Lord had freed the people from slavery in Egypt to possess the hills and plains of Canaan. So God instructed Moses to send twelve spies on a reconnaissance mission. What obstacles lay before them? What tribes might oppose them?

The spies returned, and ten of them gave a negative report: The fruit was abundant, but so were the hostile people who held the land. The majority report of the group advised that the Israelites should stop short of the conquest that was their birthright.

But there was a minority report, too. Joshua and Caleb, who had a supernatural outlook, were not concerned about risks and took no counsel of fear. These men focused on obedience to God. Caleb spoke up. "Let's go at once to take the land," he said. "We can certainly conquer it!" (Numbers 13:30).

But the majority was insistent. "They spread discouraging reports about the land among the Israelites: 'The land we explored will swallow up any who go to live there. All the people we saw were huge. We even saw giants there, the descendants of Anak. We felt like grasshoppers next to them, and that's what we looked like to them!'" (Numbers 13:32–33).

Wonderful rewards loomed just within the nation's reach. God had already performed many miracles in providing for them. Yet most of the people would not move forward in faith—and we are little different today. It is sad to realize most modern people see themselves as grasshoppers. They take counsel of their doubts rather than their faith.

> *We are commanded to live differently, "for we walk by faith, not by sight" (2 Corinthians 5:7).*

We are commanded to live differently, "for we walk by faith, not by sight" (2 Corinthians 5:7 NKJV). Ten of Israel's spies walked by sight, while Joshua and Caleb walked by faith. They ignored the obstacles, for why worry about obstacles when God has already given His assurance?

My friend, we need not live as timid grasshoppers. The Lord wants to empower you to help change the world. He wants to equip you to take on the giants of your land and bring glory to His name in your victory. He wants you to be a recipient of the grandest marching orders ever issued: the Great Commission to help win this world for Jesus Christ. Do not go timidly where God leads boldly.

Many years ago I wanted to remind myself not to fall into the trap of natural thinking like the ten spies. So I put a sign on my desk that stated, "I am no grasshopper!" With God, I have all the resources I need to make a difference in this world.

Do the challenges of life make *you* feel like a grasshopper? You can be a giant with God. Start thinking supernaturally today, and God will fill your mind with ideas of what you can do for Him through His power.

At this point, it may seem that supernatural thinking is merely about being open to God, not about our *doing* anything at all. That is not so. Our part in supernatural thinking includes the following actions:

trusting God supernaturally,

praying supernaturally,

planning supernaturally,

loving others supernaturally, and

expecting God to act supernaturally.

Let us look at each of these actions in turn, starting with how to trust God supernaturally.

—————◆—————

SUPERNATURAL THINKING IS NOT POSSIBLE APART
FROM THE SPIRIT-FILLED LIFE.

—————————

PART TWO

Acting on Supernatural Thoughts

———————❖———————

IF WE ARE GOING TO BE SUPERNATURAL THINKERS
AND LAUNCH INTO IMPORTANT SERVICE TO GOD,
WE MUST BEGIN BY DEPENDING UPON OUR
SUPERNATURAL POWER SOURCE: GOD'S SPIRIT.

———————————

5

Trusting God Supernaturally

Whater could be more basic to the believer than trusting God day by day? Yet I find that most Christians rely on their own human efforts to live up to God's standards. This is a struggle that always ends in defeat and frustration. Our gracious Lord never meant for us to attempt in our feeble abilities what He can do through us with His unlimited supernatural power.

One day I gave a talk in Portland, Oregon, about how to be filled with the Holy Spirit. At the conclusion of my talk, a man came rushing down the aisle. "This is the greatest thing I have ever heard in my life!" he began. "Today I have been liberated!" This man was no newcomer to the faith but a prosperous business executive who sat on the boards of a dozen Christian organizations. He exclaimed: "I have been trying to serve God so diligently that I practically ignored my business and my family. I have been trying to serve God in the energy of the flesh. I understand now why I have been so miserable and so unproductive!"

We all want to live the supernatural life. We desire to

think supernaturally, to plan supernaturally, to pray supernaturally, to love supernaturally, and to let our lives in every way be living proof of the supernatural power of God. Why, then, do we often fail? The answer lies in our refusal to yield to the Holy Spirit. If we are going to be supernatural thinkers and launch into important service to God, we must begin by depending upon our supernatural power source: God's Spirit. Instead, we are filled with worldliness (also called *carnality*), which I believe is at the root of virtually all Christian failure. It is essential that we learn to let God live and work supernaturally within us.

Before we can discover the secret of the Spirit-filled life, we need to understand our primary options for how to live each day.

The Bible teaches us that every life falls into one of three broad categories: the self-directed life, the Christ-directed life, and the carnal life.

THE SELF-DIRECTED LIFE

Since the rebellion of Adam and Eve (recorded in the third chapter of Genesis), we have all been born into the life of sin. That is, left to ourselves, we will choose to serve ourselves rather than God. As Isaiah said, "All of us have strayed away like sheep. We have left God's paths to follow our own" (Isaiah 53:6).

Such people will not naturally see the wisdom of living under Christ's lordship. As Paul explained in his first letter to the church at Corinth, "People who aren't Christians can't understand these truths from God's Spirit. It all sounds foolish to them because only those who have the Spirit can understand what the Spirit means" (2:14).

Such persons are completely directed by selfish concerns. Every problem in the world arises from our basic human rebellion against the perfect love and leadership of our Sovereign Lord.

We have an alternative to this self-defeating existence, and it is the Christ-directed life.

THE CHRIST-DIRECTED LIFE

We accept the free gift of salvation through Christ's atoning blood. But we do more than simply take what has been given to us; in loving gratitude, we offer ourselves as gifts in return. We place ourselves under His lordship and control.

Now, rather than living for self, we live for Christ. We are transformed so that His desires become our desires and His thoughts

> *We are transformed so that His desires become our desires and His thoughts become our thoughts.*

become our thoughts. "We can understand these things, for we have the mind of Christ" (1 Corinthians 2:16). All things begin to come into harmony for us because we are no longer striving against the grain of our godly design. We find the joy and abundance that result from serving a perfect, loving Lord.

And how does He direct our lives? The answer, of course, is that He guides us through His indwelling Spirit. This is why supernatural thinking is not possible apart from the Spirit-filled life.

Most of us grasp these two alternatives—the self-directed versus Christ-directed life. But we are left with this troubling observation: We all know believers whose lives seem as empty and frustrating as those of the nonbelievers around them. How do we account for this discrepancy?

THE CARNAL LIFE

A third kind of life has elements of both of the above. It has Christ in it, and yet it is self-directed. This is a *carnal life*, or a life lived according to the sinful nature called "the flesh."

Persons living a carnal life do not have Christ sitting on the throne of their life. Such people have accepted Christ's salvation but not His lordship. Therefore, their life remains selfish in its focus and frustrating in its result. Sin still abounds, and Christ's desires and mind-set are not evident. Here is Paul's description of the carnal life, as given to that same church in Corinth:

> Dear brothers and sisters, when I was with you I couldn't talk to you as I would to mature Christians. I had to talk as though you belonged to this world or as though you were infants in the Christian life. I had to feed you with milk and not with solid food, because you couldn't handle anything stronger. And you still aren't ready, for you are still controlled by your own sinful desires. You are jealous of one another and quarrel with each other. Doesn't that prove you are controlled by your own desires? You are acting like people who don't belong to the Lord.
>
> 1 CORINTHIANS 3:1–3

Here, then, it finally becomes clear why most of us fail to think, to plan, to love, and to live supernaturally: We say we have accepted Christ as Savior, but we have not submitted to Him as Lord—the King on the throne of our hearts. The Spirit lives within us, but He is confined to the corners of our thoughts and feelings. We are neither filled nor empowered by Him.

Our loving Savior wants so much more for us. He desires for His love and wisdom and power to flow into us as life flows from a vine to its branches. Our connection should be just as perfect, just as dependent. Jesus said, "I am the vine; you are the branches. Those who remain in me, and I in them, will produce much fruit. For apart from me you can do nothing" (John 15:5).

We "remain in" Jesus by living according to the Holy Spirit. The Spirit is "the Spirit of Christ" (Romans 8:9). And when we are controlled and empowered by the Holy Spirit as we are commanded in Acts 1:8, we will be faithful and fruitful witnesses for Christ. In fact, the eye of our mind will focus on those who do not know Jesus as Savior and Lord. The prayers of our lips will claim their salvation and expect the power to present God's wonderful plan of salvation to them. We will expect to see an awesome fruit orchard of new lives growing in Christ.

I believe most Christians do not realize how to experience the filling of the Holy Spirit. They may realize that at the moment of spiritual rebirth, when they accepted Christ as their personal Savior, the Spirit came to live within them as their permanent guest. But they have failed to consider the fact that the *presence* and the *precedence* of the Spirit are two separate issues.

We want Him to be more than present; we want Him to take precedence over every other consideration or influence.

This is why, over the years, I have invested a considerable portion of myself—through my words, teaching times, and writings—to stressing the importance of the person and ministry of the Holy Spirit and the power of the Spirit-filled life. No wonder so many men and women have come to me over the years, expressing amazement and wonder at how different their lives became with this discovery. They had simply not realized how different life can be. No more prolonged spiritual emptiness! No more of the frustration of empty religion without godly relationship! No more of the despair of trying to live a powerful supernatural life by using weak natural resources!

How, then, can we live such a life?

EMBRACE THE POWER

Those who have come to me with great smiles on their faces, telling me how different their lives had become, were most delighted to discover that being filled with the Holy Spirit was a process that could happen immediately. You need not wait for months or years or decades to experience such a filling. You can experience the unlimited abundance and fruitfulness of the Spirit-filled life today—right now. The steps are clear and simple:

> *The* presence *and the* precedence *of the Spirit are two separate issues.*

THIRSTY?

Jesus invites, "If you are thirsty, come to me! If you believe in me, come and drink! For the Scriptures declare that rivers of living water will flow out from within" (John 7:37–38). When He said "living water," He was speaking of the Spirit, who would be given to everyone believing in Him. You must begin by being thirsty for the living water that only Christ can offer.

CONFESS YOUR SINS

This is actually an occasion for joy—God has forgiven every one of your sins! By confessing them, you consign them to His atonement through the precious blood of Christ shed on the cross. Through God's mighty power, you separate yourself from the power those sins have held over you and the power they would hold in the future. "You were dead because of your sins and because your sinful nature was not yet cut away. Then God made you alive with Christ. He forgave all our sins. He canceled the record that contained the charges against us. He took it and destroyed it by nailing it to Christ's cross" (Colossians 2:13–14). Therefore, "if we confess our sins to him, he is faithful and just to forgive us and to cleanse us from every wrong" (1 John 1:9).

> ❖
>
> *You can experience the unlimited abundance and fruitfulness of the Spirit-filled life today—right now.*

SURRENDER EVERY AREA OF YOUR LIFE TO GOD

Romans 12:1–2 reads,

> Dear brothers and sisters, I plead with you to give your bodies to God. Let them be a living and holy sacrifice—the kind he will accept. When you think of what he has done for you, is this too much to ask? Don't copy the behavior and customs of this world, but let God transform you into a new person by changing the way you think. Then you will know what God wants you to do, and you will know how good and pleasing and perfect his will really is.

This, so tragically, is the step where most Christians fail. They fail to totally give themselves over to the loving and perfect lordship of Christ. It is essential that you come before His throne and lay *every* aspect of your life—desires, hopes, dreams, gifts, and shortcomings—before Him. Your entire life and being are to constitute a living sacrifice. It is then that you may begin to think supernaturally, to live and to love supernaturally, to make supernatural plans, and to expect supernatural results. It is then that you will finally break the chains that bind you to the hopeless ways of worldliness. Give in to the lordship of Christ.

By Faith, Claim the Fullness of the Holy Spirit

After all, God has not offered the filling of His Spirit as an option; He has *commanded* it. "Let the Holy Spirit fill and control you" (Ephesians 5:18). We claim His promise to answer any prayer offered according to His will: "We can be confident that he will listen to us whenever we ask him for anything in line with his will. And if we know he is listening when we make our requests, we can be sure that he will give us what we ask for" (1 John 5:14–15). It is certainly His will and His command that we submit to the wonderful filling of the Holy Spirit. It only remains to ask and to know that He will answer.

If you, like so many people, have never yielded to the Spirit's filling and to His full control, I suggest that you offer words such as the following to our Lord:

> *My Lord and my Savior, how true it is—the filling of Your Spirit makes all the difference. Without Your daily power and guidance, my life is no different from those of the nonbelievers of this world. Yet Your Word assures me that if I invite You to have Your perfect way in my life, I can live the supernatural life and achieve the impossible for You and Your glory. I acknowledge my sinfulness and brokenness. I accept*

*the gift of Your forgiveness through the precious,
atoning blood of Your only begotten Son on the cross.
And today I affirm the lordship of Christ, that very
Son, over every aspect of my existence. I will not with-
hold any thought, any desire, any temptation or plan
from His loving control. Now, by faith, I claim the
fullness of the Holy Spirit. I thirst for the living water
that alone can satisfy my soul. I claim Your loving
promise as I obey Your sovereign command. I thank
You and praise You for filling me and for the great
work You will do within me and through me, beginning this very moment. Amen.*

If you take God at His word, He will certainly take you at
yours. He will fill you and empower you with the incredible
presence and power of the Holy Spirit, and from that moment
on, your life will not be even remotely the same. You will know
joy. You will know vitality and new energy. You will share the
gospel and win people to the Lord with a confidence and
power you never thought possible. You will know abundance in
every aspect of daily life. But most of all, you will experience
the invasion of the supernatural into the depths of your soul.

With the Spirit in your life, your prayers will align themselves with the will of God as you seek His help to live out the
design He has for you.

———————— ❖ ————————

"THEREFORE I TELL YOU, WHATEVER YOU ASK
FOR IN PRAYER, BELIEVE THAT YOU HAVE
RECEIVED IT, AND IT WILL BE YOURS."

—JESUS CHRIST

6

Praying Supernaturally

After putting on EXPLO '72, Campus Crusade for Christ emerged in sound financial condition with the exception of one category: the TV expenses. We incurred a net loss of over $1 million on broadcast costs. Seeking to be responsible stewards, we attempted to raise the money to pay our bills. But with each passing month, we still could not meet our obligations. So I wrote a letter to our creditors, assuring them that we were fully committed to paying the principal and that, in the meantime, we would be paying just the interest on the amount we owed. Still the funds did not appear. For a year our ministry strained under this financial burden. Finally, at a Campus Crusade for Christ board meeting one Saturday, I led the board in prayer as we laid our financial need before the Lord.

The following Tuesday I received an unexpected phone call from a businessman I did not know. His name was Bud Miller. He told me how our ministry and materials had changed his life when, years before, he had received a *Four Spiritual Laws* pamphlet and my booklet on the Holy Spirit.

After reading them, he had bowed in prayer to receive Christ as his Savior and to ask the Holy Spirit to fill and control him. Mr. Miller had attended our Lay Institute for Evangelism at Arrowhead Springs, California, and he was sharing his faith regularly. To my amazement, he even told me that my picture was hanging on his office wall! It so happened that Mr. Miller had recently made a property sale in his business and had on hand $1.1 million, which God had impressed upon him to present to us. "I am certain you will know what to do with this money," he said. That, of course, was an understatement! We knew exactly what to do with the money—it covered the sum we owed for our TV expenses and interest, to the dollar.

> *We only had to ask for what we needed in a spirit of dependence upon God, claiming His gracious promises.*

I am persuaded that we received God's support because we were working in God's will. We only had to ask for what we needed in a spirit of dependence upon God, claiming His gracious promises. He has never let us down, and He never will. We can pray supernaturally and know that He will supply our needs according to His own all-wise timing. In this way, He enables us to fulfill the vision He has given us through supernatural thinking.

THE SECRET OF ANSWERED PRAYER

The promises of Jesus that most amaze and puzzle us are the ones that require believing God for the impossible. I believe this is true because we are so far removed from the lifestyle of faith He desires us to live. Jesus spoke to His disciples as if they should live and work in exactly the same way He did—as if they should be able to accomplish the miraculous, cast out demons, and serve the needy in astonishing ways. Though He was the divine Son of God, He encouraged His human followers to seek His own perfection.

Matthew 21:21–22 confounds many people: "I assure you, if you have faith and don't doubt, you can do things like this and much more. You can even say to this mountain, 'May God lift you up and throw you into the sea,' and it will happen. If you believe, you will receive whatever you ask for in prayer."

The disciples were amazed by what they had just witnessed: Jesus had caused a fig tree to wither. But Jesus wanted them to understand that such miracles were not limited to Himself. He immediately named a much greater one—the tossing of a mountain into the sea—and said that it would happen "if you have faith and don't doubt."

Readers tend to make a mistake about the meaning of Jesus' promise. They assume that moving a mountain is a matter of working as hard as they can to believe something, pushing the doubt out of their minds by sheer force of will. They wrongly assume it is the insistence of the believer that empowers the miracle. This, of course, is wrong—and it also does not work!

Supernatural thinking is not about the force of our human effort to believe something; rather, it is built from our first-hand knowledge of the God who is the object of our belief. A miracle happens not because we *will* it to happen but because God *wishes* it to happen—and because the believer knows he or she can trust completely in Him and His promises. That believer has taken on the mind of Christ, so that he or she agrees with the Lord on what should be done. And knowing this is God's will, the person has perfect faith and no doubt.

This is why supernatural thinking must precede supernatural prayer. As Paul expressed it, "I know whom I have believed and am persuaded that He is able to keep what I

---❖---

A miracle happens not because we will it to happen but because God wishes it to happen.

have committed to Him until that Day" (2 Timothy 1:12 NKJV). We know the One whom we have believed. We build our faith in God through knowing Him and coming to know His purposes. Then we pray in His will with perfect confidence.

The secret of answered prayer, then, is not in how forcefully we believe but in how intimately we know God. Knowing and loving Him, we come to see the mountains He wants us to move. Then we need not struggle to believe, for we know Him well, we have seen His faithfulness, and we know His faithfulness is as infinite as the task seems impossible.

PRAYING WITH THE HEART OF CHRIST

If the secret of supernatural thinking is to put on the mind of Christ, the secret of supernatural praying is to talk to God with the heart of Christ. The pattern holds true.

Mark 1:35 tells us, "Jesus awoke long before daybreak and went out alone into the wilderness to pray." Even after a long day of ministry, He would awake early so that He might be alone with His beloved Father. Jesus knew that His strength came from His union with the Father.

When Jesus taught His disciples to pray, He gave them this model prayer:

"Our Father in heaven,

Hallowed be Your name.

Your kingdom come.

Your will be done

On earth as it is in heaven.

Give us this day our daily bread.

And forgive us our debts,

As we forgive our debtors.

And do not lead us into temptation,

But deliver us from the evil one.

For Yours is the kingdom and the power and the glory

forever. Amen."

MATTHEW 6:9–13 NKJV

At the opening of the Lord's Prayer, Jesus praises the Father, worships His name, and expresses His willingness for God's kingdom and will to be established. In other words, He is aligning His own will with that of the Father, praying that every event will transpire "on earth as it is in heaven." Similarly, as we bring our will in line with God's will, we bring this world in line with God's kingdom. Then the doors of heaven are thrown open and supernatural events may take place on earth.

Perhaps the most moving of all of Jesus' recorded prayers is the one He prayed in the garden of Gethsemane during the hours leading up to His arrest. In this prayer we see how He approached the Father in a time of great inner turmoil and anguish. "O My Father, if it is possible, let this cup pass from Me; nevertheless, not as I will, but as You will" (Matthew 26:39 NKJV). Jesus poured out His heart honestly to His Father, but at the same time He affirmed the Father's will is the only will that should prevail.

We, too, can approach our loving Father and tell Him how we feel. Yet as we pray, as we spend time in His majestic presence, He will give us courage. He will help us put aside our imperfect and shortsighted will in favor of His will, which is always perfect and eternally sighted. He will give us the resolve to do what we need to do, even when it seems impossible. Jesus left that dark garden to achieve the most supernatural goal ever conceived—He died so that the human race could be liberated from sin and rebellion. It came to pass because He prayed in the will of His Father.

PRAYER FOR THE IMPOSSIBLE

Arming ourselves with the mind of Christ leads to a habit of prayer with the heart of Christ. Just as Jesus aligned Himself with the will of the Father through prayer, so we, in praying, find ourselves more and more at the center of His will. We abide with Him more frequently. As He works in us to will what He wills, we ask greater requests of Him in the confidence that they are the results He wants. And, finally, we see greater miracles take place all around us. A goal that seemed impossible in the past becomes a reality because God wants it and because it glorifies His name.

One of the most amazing people of prayer in history was a supernatural thinker by the name of George Müller, who founded several Christian orphanages in the nineteenth century. Müller believed that only God could supply the needs of his ministry, and he devoted himself completely to prayer so that he might depend totally upon God to provide. In five great houses he provided for two thousand boys and girls, yet he never personally asked donors to supply food, clothing, repairs, or any other need that might emerge. Time after time, some unlikely event would come to pass that would cause Müller's need to be met, often at the last moment.

One night, for example, he retired to bed with the knowledge that his cupboards were bare. It appeared there would be no breakfast for his children the following morning. Of course, he prayed about it: "Give us this day our daily bread." Then Müller got a good night's sleep, for he knew that his ministry was in the hands of God.

George Müller was a man who thought with the mind of Christ and prayed with the heart of Christ.

The next morning Müller rose at his usual early hour and took a walk. He came across a friend, and the two men began to talk. Müller's friend suddenly mentioned that he had a contribution for the orphanage. He said, "I've been meaning to give you this money." Müller smiled as he accepted the generous donation, but he was not the least bit surprised. He had asked God, and God had once again been faithful.

On another occasion there was a closer call. Müller had the children wash their hands and sit down for their meal even though there was no food. At that moment a meat cart broke down outside the orphanage door. The driver knocked and told Müller that he had a cart full of meat that would spoil if not eaten soon. The children ate well that morning.

During his lifetime, George Müller kept a prayer log in which he listed the date, his request, and God's answer as it came. The list grew to ten thousand answered prayers! Surely this was a man who thought with the mind of Christ and prayed with the heart of Christ. He saw every detail of life with an uncompromised faith perspective, and he claimed God's promises at every opportunity. Therefore, he experienced the joy of God's miracles on almost a daily basis.

I have experienced thousands of answers to prayer and am convinced that God is faithful to His promises. But you must find that out for yourself. You will need to assign a time and a place for being alone with your heavenly Father daily, or you will never come to know Him intimately. The rewards of a disciplined prayer life are endless. Pray in God's will and live in His glory as He brings miracle upon miracle to pass.

Our gracious heavenly Father is calling upon you today to enter into intimate friendship with Him. "Call to Me, and I will answer you," He says, "and show you great and mighty things, which you do not know" (Jeremiah 33:3 NKJV). "Great and mighty things"—that is another way of referring to impossible things or supernatural blessings. I pray that you are eager to see the blessings God has reserved for you.

7

Planning Supernaturally

In the early 1980s the worldwide ministry of Campus Crusade for Christ was growing rapidly—in fact, exponentially. Our great dream of that period was to hold a worldwide student congress attended by at least thirty thousand students representing each country of the world. In 1983, we calculated the financial cost of such an endeavor would be $2,000 per student, or a total of $60 million. The idea of putting on such an event was outlandish in human terms—the word for it would be *impossible*. Making this dream a reality would require the supernatural work of God. And we trusted it was His will.

Much of the burden for planning this event fell upon our international vice president, Bailey Marks. One morning, as Bailey was shaving, he blurted out to the Lord, "God, what do You want me to do?"

Bailey heard God inaudibly tell him, "Bailey, you are going about this the wrong way. Rather than bringing the people to the conference, you need to take the conference to people all over the world."

Bailey asked God how that could be accomplished, and he believed that the Lord said, "By satellite."

Bailey told the Lord that he did not know a thing about satellites. But there was no response, and Bailey realized the Lord expected him to figure it out himself.

As Bailey stood in my office excitedly telling me what had happened, I looked down at my desk and received confirmation that this was the work of God. My eyes were resting on a business card that had been handed to me at a speaking engagement in Phoenix, Arizona, the day before. Michael Clifford wanted to start a business that would conduct satellite conferences through hotels.

Before the week was out, Bailey, Michael, and I were meeting, praying, and planning for a great work of the Lord that turned out to be EXPLO '85, the largest closed-circuit satellite conference that had ever been conducted to date. We had originally spoken of thirty thousand students and a cost of $60 million. Instead, the numbers increased tenfold to three hundred thousand students and laypeople in ninety-four locations on every continent at a cost of slightly less than $7 million. God is truly astounding!

Without supernaturally thinking people of God such as Bailey Marks, there would be no miracles like EXPLO '85. Small plans do not enflame minds and hearts. Ambitious, visionary, *supernatural* plans, however, do capture the imagination.

Over decades of ministry, God has impressed upon me many visions for service to Him. If I had moved forward with "natural," human-centered planning, none of those visions would ever have been fulfilled. Our Lord gives us dreams and visions of the impossible, and they can be fulfilled only in the supernatural power of God. This is why we must not only think and pray supernaturally, but also boldly make plans with faith in God. If it is God's will, there is nothing we cannot plan to accomplish and pursue in God's power. Our plans for Christ and His kingdom should be so big that without His supernatural help, they would surely fail.

How Great Works Come to Be

It has been said that those who fail to plan plan to fail. The converse is also true: Those who succeed at planning plan to succeed. I have met many Christians who seem to possess all the ingredients for success, but they lack the right recipe. Another word for a recipe, of course, is a *plan*. Fine ingredients might produce a poor supper in the hands of a careless or inexperienced cook, but in the hands of a master chef those same ingredients will become a dinner fit for a king. And God does indeed wish the production of our lives to be fit for the King. Not only must we be faithful and obedient, but also we must use the mind He has given us to plan wisely.

Many Christians seem to possess all the ingredients for success, but they lack the right recipe.

"God has not given us a spirit of fear, but of power and of love and of *a sound mind*" (2 Timothy 1:7 NKJV). With their sound, supernaturally influenced minds, godly planners often come up with new and even surprising ways to accomplish great things for God. That was true for Bailey Marks and his groundbreaking use of satellite technology. It has been true for many others.

From the beginning of Campus Crusade for Christ International, we have recognized the place of wise planning. If we had not carefully prayed and thoughtfully planned at every step of our expansion from one campus chapter to a global movement, I am certain that God would never have honored and empowered our work. All along the way we have been blessed by the gifted insight and foresight of many of the brightest minds of our time—I wish there were space in this book to name them all.

Experience proves that if we seek to live supernaturally for God, we must think with the mind of Christ, love with the heart of Christ, and pray in the power of the Holy Spirit. Then, when the time comes, we must begin to draw up the blueprint and lay out the path. If we look too far ahead, we may become discouraged and frightened. But as we plan carefully, one step at a time, we will eventually build a stairway to the wonderful dreams God has given us.

> *If we want to be supernatural thinkers, we need God's wisdom in our plans.*

GUIDELINES FOR WISE PLANNING

Perhaps the wisest planner in history was Solomon, for whom God reserved the task of building the temple in Jerusalem. You may remember that David had the dream of being that architect, but God had Solomon, David's son, in mind for the massive undertaking. This structure was to be a testimony in stone to the awesome and holy presence of God. Solomon, known throughout the world for his wisdom, led in the building.

Solomon created one other monument that speaks of the wisdom of planning: the biblical book of Proverbs. In that book we find many wise words on a subject for which Solomon was uniquely gifted. Let us consider three of his guidelines for godly planning.

Start with God's Plans

"Commit your work to the LORD, and then your plans will succeed" (Proverbs 16:3). We do not ask God to bless *our* plans; we go to Him first to find out what plans He wants us to have. His plans always bring glory to Him, not to us.

Why do so many wonderful projects fail? It is often because, though they seem godly and virtuous on the surface, those seeking to accomplish them are driven by the wrong motives.

As you think and pray to fulfill supernatural goals for God, be certain from the beginning that you are directed solely toward the goal of His glory and the advancement of His kingdom. Then, as you work for weeks, months, and even years, take a fresh inventory of your spirit and your desires from time to time. Has anything changed? Are you still as committed to loving God with all your heart, soul, mind, and strength as you were in the beginning?

I need not remind you that the Evil One will attempt to pervert your motivations and desires along the way. Even Solomon, as wise as he was, eventually compromised himself through marrying wives who did not honor God. As a result, he brought tragedy and heartbreak not only to himself and those who were close to him, but to the rest of the nation as well.

Ask for God's Wisdom

"We can gather our thoughts, but the LORD gives the right answer" (Proverbs 16:1). Our accumulated wisdom is an insignificant speck before the all-knowing mind of our great Creator God. If we want to be supernatural thinkers, we need God's wisdom in our plans (see James 1:5).

Never completely trust your own insight and calculations, for many times they will fail, though you may mean well. On the other hand, God has the right answer on every occasion, and according to Proverbs 16:1, He gives it to us. So gather your thoughts, but at the same time seek God's perfect and infallible wisdom at every turn.

———❖———

If you want to see results, you will need plans constructed with the wisdom of God.

Let me also remind you that the greatest part of God's wisdom for our needs is already contained in His precious Word, the Bible. Search it constantly, know it intimately, and memorize it faithfully. Then your heart will overflow with His answers to many questions.

REALIZE GOD IS IN CONTROL

"We can make our plans, but the LORD determines our steps" (Proverbs 16:9). We cannot afford to let our plans become rigid; rather, we must keep walking with the Spirit and listening for Him to tell us of adjustments He might want us to make to our plans. All along the way, He is in control.

This realization provides a welcome source of protection and security. We need never be anxious when our dreams seem to be in jeopardy or heartbroken when they seem to have run aground. We know that God is sovereign, and we know that while our plans are flawed, His perfect plan never fails. I have found all three of these guidelines to be proved true in my own experience.

SURVIVING THE STORMS

Our experience in ministry has always been that a detailed plan, wise in foresight, is like an umbrella that protects us from unexpected storms. We must take into consideration not only our preferred scenario but also the one that would take effect in the worst case. Our Lord Jesus Christ said:

"Don't begin until you count the cost. For who would begin construction of a building without first getting estimates and then checking to see if there is enough money to pay the bills? Otherwise, you might complete only the foundation before running out of funds. And then how everyone would laugh at you! They would say, 'There's the person who started that building and ran out of money before it was finished!'"

LUKE 14:28–30

Clearly Jesus was telling us it is wise and prudent to plan ahead and to master the details. A builder who prepares for the future is protected from failure, ridicule, and the heartbreak of spoiled dreams. Storms will certainly come. There will be times when those who think and plan "in the flesh" (through the limits of human capabilities) surely would give in to what seems impossible. But the supernatural planner keeps on believing. He or she knows that God has never failed and never will—and this person is willing to take the supernatural step of faithful planning.

In 1945, I had a vision to produce and distribute a film about the life of Jesus that could be used for evangelistic purposes worldwide. This was not a vision I could have dreamed up on my own; it clearly came from God. But the vision had to wait for its fulfillment until the 1970s, when I assigned an excellent planner named Paul Eshleman to the *JESUS* film project.

Paul had been a part of our organization since 1966 and had served Christ with consistent excellence. He had done an amazing job in handling the logistics of EXPLO '72 in Dallas. He had coordinated the Here's Life America "I Found It" campaign in 1976. By this time, he was our U.S. field director. He had been faithful in small things and in greater ones, a reflection of the servant in Jesus' parable found in Matthew 25:14–30.

Could Campus Crusade for Christ International afford to lend such a gifted servant to a brand-new, risky venture? We could if we were serious about supernatural thinking and supernatural planning. Otherwise, we would be like the faithless servant in Matthew 25—the one who failed to aggressively, faithfully invest the resources given to him by his master. I knew we could not afford to play it safe. After all, the vision for the *JESUS* film was not a human one but a godly, supernatural, "impossible" one. It demanded the best we had to offer, including our best human resources.

After the film was completed, Paul was the one who worked out the extraordinary plan to get the film into every corner of the globe. His plan was complicated and detailed, but it has been marvelously successful. I believe that, should the Lord Jesus Christ wait a few more years before His return, the film will be translated into every language on the face of the earth, so that everyone within reach of a film projector, a computer, a VCR or DVD player, or some other communication medium will have the opportunity to hear the saving gospel of Jesus Christ.

Never forget this: You can be the boldest of visionaries and possess the deepest faith, but if you want to see results, you will need plans constructed with the wisdom of God. If we are to become supernatural thinkers, we must know how to be supernatural planners.

8

Loving Supernaturally

Earlier in this book, I introduced to you Dr. Joon Gon Kim, the man who accepted God's earthshaking vision for him and dared to think and plan supernaturally in South Korea. He believes God has called South Korean Christians to reach the whole world with the gospel, and Korean churches are among the fastest growing in North America. What I did not mention until now is that Dr. Kim is a man of supernatural faith because he is a man of supernatural love. His personal story is one of the most amazing I have ever heard.

One evening in 1950, communist guerrillas in Korea invaded Dr. Kim's village, killing everyone in their path including Dr. Kim's wife and father. Dr. Kim was beaten severely and left for dead. When he returned to consciousness, he took his daughter in his arms and fled to the mountains. Over the next few weeks, father and daughter were hungry and lacked shelter, but Dr. Kim had time to think.

He knew that the Bible said Jesus died to save everyone, including Dr. Kim. Somehow his mind kept returning to Jesus, a man who, like Dr. Kim, had been beaten and tortured—to the point of death, in Jesus' case. The difference was that Jesus held no bitterness in His heart. He loved the very ones who beat Him, mocked Him, and condemned Him to a shameful and torturous death. His love conquered hatred, and He rose to live again.

Dr. Kim reflected on those facts, and suddenly his heart was filled with the peace and love of Christ. From that moment on, he was no longer bitter. The Spirit of God immediately placed in Dr. Kim's heart a strong desire to return to the village and seek out the communist chief who had led the attack. His objective was not one of revenge but one of forgiveness. His burden was to tell the man that he loved him—and to share his faith in Christ.

Are you capable of loving people who have hurt you?

When Dr. Kim walked through the communist leader's door, the chief must have thought he was a ghost! Dr. Kim was presumed dead. But after a few short moments, the communist chief and the Christian—predator and prey—were kneeling together in the love of their Savior. After the chief became a Christian, the two men made plans to lead other communists to Christ. And that is exactly what they did. Dr. Kim helped to build a church for nearly two hundred communist converts whom they led into God's kingdom.

My friend, are you capable of such love for the lost? Are you capable of loving people who have hurt you? People who are unlovable? People who reject you?

Supernatural thinking is all about ministry, and ministry is all about people. So supernatural thinking will inevitably involve us in situations where we are called upon to deal with people we find difficult, demanding, or unpleasant. It is then that we must be able to love supernaturally.

THE LOVE OF GOD IN OUR HEARTS

Even with a mind set on eternal things and a prayer life empowered by the Holy Spirit, we are challenged to love others when to do so seems impossible. This is a battle we cannot afford to lose, for the inability to love will undermine the accomplishments and goals upon which we have set our hearts. We need to be filled with love.

Everyone is capable of love of some sort. However, the love to which we as believers are called is of a special kind. Jesus said:

> "You have heard that the law of Moses says, 'Love your neighbor' and hate your enemy. But I say, love your enemies! Pray for those who persecute you! ... If you love only those who love you, what good is that? Even corrupt tax collectors do that much. If you are kind only to your friends, how are you different from anyone else? Even pagans do that. But you are to be perfect, even as your Father in heaven is perfect."
>
> MATTHEW 5:43–48

The godless love naturally, but the godly love supernaturally.

If you experience the transforming love of God, His love will fill you to overflowing. As Jesus Christ forgave His tormentors, so you will find it possible to forgive those who hurt you. Though the world will never understand, you will be filled with a love that makes you capable of recognizing that vengeance belongs to the Lord and to Him alone.

The Lord's Prayer contains these words: "Forgive us our sins, just as we have forgiven those who have sinned against us" (Matthew 6:12). We must never forget, then, that God has interwoven the forgiveness we receive with the forgiveness we offer to others. Simply put, God will not forgive us if we refuse to forgive others. An unforgiving heart is proof that we have not fully accepted the love and forgiveness of Christ. For when we do embrace His loving mercy, we pass it on to others, as Dr. Kim did.

> *If you experience the transforming love of God, His love will fill you to overflowing.*

The word generally used for love in the New Testament is *agape,* referring to a selfless, unconditional love. Paul helps us understand in greater detail what this kind of love looks like in the following passage.

> Love is patient and kind. Love is not jealous or boastful or proud or rude. Love does not demand its own way. Love is not irritable, and it keeps no record of when it has been wronged. It is never glad about injustice but rejoices whenever the truth wins out. Love never gives up, never loses faith, is always hopeful, and endures through every circumstance.
>
> 1 CORINTHIANS 13:4–7

As you read those words, you might think, *This describes an impossible love. I could never live up to such a standard!*

And you would be correct. Who is able to love like that?

I believe you know the answer to that question—nobody but our wonderful Lord and Savior could love like that. That is why our only hope is to cast ourselves completely upon Him and invite the Holy Spirit to fill and empower us to love in a supernatural way. In humble faith we will be filled with a love that is far above the natural, worldly variety. It will be a love against which the world can have no defense, for it confounds all expectations. It will overcome any barrier.

Through such a love as this, God will accomplish supernatural goals through you. And believe it or not, you can love anyone in this way—by faith.

How to Love the Unlovable

For many years I have devoted myself to loving others *by faith*, and whenever possible I have used speaking engagements, writing, and personal friendships to help others understand this concept.

Few people comprehend that we have the potential to love anyone God puts in our path. A husband may say he has lost the love he once had for his wife. I would immediately advise him to claim God's unconditional love, *by faith*, to flow through him to his wife. He will then discover a love that springs back into flame, rekindled by the love of our Savior. You may say to me, "I simply cannot love my boss!" No, you cannot—not in your own sinful striving. But God has always loved and will always love perfectly. He wants to love that boss through you, and you need only ask Him and trust Him. You cannot offer me the name of any person on this earth, no matter what he or she has done to you, whom you cannot love by faith, through the enabling of the Holy Spirit.

We can summarize this profound principle by affirming five truths:

1. GOD LOVES US UNCONDITIONALLY

There is nothing in the world we could ever do to deserve the tiniest fraction of God's love. He loves us because He is love and because we are His children. He loves us despite every weakness or sin within us. He loves us enough to provide a way for victory over sin and its punishment, through the blood of His only begotten Son on the cross.

Such love is the most wonderful power in the universe. Paul wrote:

> I am convinced that nothing can ever separate us from his love. Death can't, and life can't. The angels can't, and the demons can't. Our fears for today, our worries about tomorrow, and even the powers of hell can't keep God's love away. Whether we are high above the sky or in the deepest ocean, nothing in all creation will ever be able to separate us from the love of God that is revealed in Christ Jesus our Lord.
>
> ROMANS 8:38–39

We may never comprehend such a love, but we can humbly accept it and experience it.

2. WE ARE COMMANDED TO LOVE

Jesus said, "'You must love the Lord your God with all your heart, all your soul, and all your mind.' This is the first and greatest commandment. A second is equally important: 'Love your neighbor as yourself.' All the other commandments and all the demands of the prophets are based on these two commandments" (Matthew 22:37–40).

Those who are properly related to God on the vertical plane will be properly related to others on the horizontal plane.

Walking in the Spirit, in other words, will help us walk in proper relationship with each other.

The apostle John wrote:

> God showed how much he loved us by sending his only
> Son into the world so that we might have eternal life
> through him. This is real love. It is not that we loved God,
> but that he loved us and sent his Son as a sacrifice to take
> away our sins. Dear friends, since God loved us that much,
> we surely ought to love each other.
>
> 1 JOHN 4:9–11

We love because God first loved us. What reasonable man or woman would choose any other response than to take that love and let it overflow to everyone we meet in this life?

3. WE CANNOT LOVE IN OUR OWN STRENGTH

If we feel overwhelmed by considering the requirements of this kind of love, our feelings are reasonable. "For the sinful nature is always hostile to God. It never did obey God's laws, and it never will. That's why those who are still under the control of their sinful nature can never please God" (Romans 8:7–8).

The powerful, selfless, and unconditional love commanded by God is unavailable to us through our frail human capabilities. We know this all too well from our own experience. Love is patient and kind and has all the other attributes found in 1 Corinthians 13, but we are not naturally patient and kind. We do not naturally love strangers, much less our enemies.

4. WE CAN LOVE WITH GOD'S LOVE

God's love is the greatest power in the universe. That love found its ultimate expression in the person and work of Jesus Christ. How does the love of God make itself known in this world? How does it respond to need? To evil? To challenges of every kind? We need only study the life and words of Jesus to find the answers.

Best of all, that love did not end when Jesus ascended to heaven to join His eternal Father. It comes into our heart the moment we receive Jesus Christ as our personal Savior. The Holy Spirit brings us that love and helps us day by day to grow into it. "He has given us the Holy Spirit to fill our hearts with his love" (Romans 5:5).

We need not struggle to love in our own limited power. God will provide all the love we need. We will find His love overflowing toward those around us, as His Spirit uses us more every day.

But how do we go about it?

5. WE LOVE BY FAITH!

We are saved through faith. We live by faith. We serve by faith. And we love by faith. Each of us will be surprised and delighted to see what God will do in us when we choose to love people by an act of faith.

Two Scripture passages are important to claim as we love by faith. The first is a command. Jesus said, "Love your enemies!" (Matthew 5:44). The second is a promise: "We can be confident that he will listen to us whenever we ask him for anything in line with his will. And if we know he is listening when we make our requests, we can be sure that he will give us what we ask for" (1 John 5:14–15).

If we put these two extraordinary passages together, we know we can love supernaturally. By faith we know that it is God's will for us to love Him, our neighbor, our brother, and our enemy. Therefore, we can and will obey His command to love as we claim His promise that He will empower us to love.

SUPERNATURAL LOVE IN ACTION

Do not think that the type of love described in this chapter is a pipe dream. I could offer you many illustrations of supernatural love from my own life. I could describe occasions when I have been forced to my knees to implore God to give me nothing but love for misguided individuals who have brought pain to my family and my ministry. I could tell you how God has provided that love, and I could describe how I have seen its evidence in the lives of my closest friends and coworkers.

I could tell you stories about others as well, such as the one about Jim Elliot and his fellow missionaries who were martyred by members of the Auca tribe in eastern Ecuador. What makes this story remarkable is that some of the missionaries' bereaved wives went to the murderers and loved

> *By faith we know it is God's will for us to love Him, our neighbor, our brother, and our enemy.*

them by faith. They prayed for the Auca and continued sharing the gospel until many of the villagers were won to Christ. That, my friend, qualifies as an "impossible" love— achievable only through supernatural means. And it accomplished an impossible, supernatural goal.

I could also tell you about Corrie ten Boom. This woman

was imprisoned at the Ravensbrück concentration camp during World War II because she hid Jews from the Nazis. She saw her beloved sister, Betsie, die in the camp while she barely escaped death herself. After the war, she traveled the world talking about forgiveness and the love of God. She even opened a rehabilitation center for Germans who worked under the Nazi regime. One day she met the guard who was most responsible for Betsie's death, and he asked for her forgiveness. Corrie said later that only by God's power was she able to shake that man's hand and forgive him. She had supernatural love for an enemy.

I could also mention someone you have probably never heard of, a quiet man who lived in China many years ago. Lough Fook took seriously the responsibilities that came with being a follower of Jesus Christ. He looked around him and saw millions of his brothers and sisters who needed to know about the amazing love of God, and he knew the time would come for him to demonstrate that love through his own life.

In those days great numbers of Chinese men were bonded in slavery and delivered to the mines of South Africa. The lives of these men were thrown away as if they had no value, for they were forced to descend into the depths of the earth where gold was mined. They worked long, sunless days deep in the caverns, with no hope to which they could cling. There was no release or any liberation short of death from suffocation, infected lungs, or the occasional cave-in—and it was never long before one of these fates delivered the Chinese slave from his life of agony.

Lough Fook had a supernatural thought. A wealthy and free man, he nevertheless placed himself on the human slave market and became a slave for a term of five years. He was loaded aboard a ship with the other slaves and made the sad voyage to South Africa. There Fook toiled in the mines for years, encouraging his brothers and talking constantly about Jesus as he worked—for that, of course, was the reason he had allowed himself to be delivered into slavery.

I cannot tell you that Lough Fook ended human slavery. I cannot tell you that his story had a happy ending—not in human terms, that is. But he accomplished something wonderful and eternal in the kingdom of heaven. Every week, one or two more believers swelled the ranks of Christian believers. Even in the blackest and deepest of earthly places, the light of Christ shone brightly and there was hope again. The day arrived when Lough Fook's own human light was snuffed out, but how that light had shone! He left behind nearly two hundred young men who had begun as slaves of the darkness and now were willing slaves of Christ.

Like Jesus Himself, as related so movingly in Philippians 2, Lough Fook had humbled himself and taken the form of a slave. He had become obedient even unto death, and he had descended into the pit out of love for his brothers. And I personally believe that, having given up all he had, he was greeted in heaven with a reception such as you and I could not begin to imagine.

> *God's kind of love does not depend upon emotions. It is an act of the will.*

Lough Fook had achieved something that seems impossible by trusting in God for a love that was unstoppable.

How could love survive in such a terrible, loveless setting as those South African mines? If love were merely an emotion or a sentiment, it could not. But God's kind of love does not depend upon emotions. It is an act of the will. Ask God to fill your heart with His love until it overflows upon those whom you might otherwise count as enemies. Then you will see your supernatural love conquer even the impossible.

The impossible—that is what God is in the business of delivering. We can believe it and look for it every day.

9

Expecting Supernatural Results

When William Carey was a young man, most Christians either ignored or lived in ignorance of the Great Commission. Today, we find it hard to believe that as late as 1790 no organized mission initiatives targeted the entire world. Few were taking seriously the command of Jesus to go into every corner of the earth with the gospel.

Carey was an exception. He was not a well-educated man, having received no formal schooling past age twelve. But after he trusted Christ as his Lord and Savior at the age of eighteen, Carey saw the urgency of going everywhere, preaching to everyone, and bending every effort toward sharing the good news of Jesus Christ. He applied himself to studying languages and in time mastered Latin, Greek, Hebrew, Italian, and Dutch.

As Carey began to meet with pastors to urge them to send missionaries, his words fell on deaf ears. Most of these men were more interested in the immediate problems of their own churches—why worry about the nonbelievers in China or

Africa? One elderly pastor impatiently told Carey that when God wanted to reach the nations, He would do it without consulting Carey or the pastor!

Carey published a book arguing that the Great Commission of Matthew 28:18–20 is a mandate for every Christian, not just the original disciples. Many believers read and embraced Carey's book. The energetic young preacher also delivered a sermon that immediately became famous. In it he called upon believers to "expect great things from God; attempt great things for God."

> *"Expect great things from God; attempt great things for God."*
> *—William Carey*

This man's supernatural dream was to see the church demonstrate a concern for every nation and to begin strenuously organizing its efforts to send missionaries in every direction. Could one man make a difference against seventeen centuries of spiritual inertia? He could if he expected great things from God and attempted great things for Him. William Carey truly lived his own personal motto. He was a man of faith, and faith makes all the difference.

Carey never became discouraged. He sought like-minded persons until finally a body of believers had taken on his vision, fallen into step behind him, and begun raising funds for mission work. In no time Carey was sent to India, where he encountered many obstacles to the spread of the gospel. Sometimes he had to fight the Indian caste system; sometimes the British government caused problems. In 1812, his printing plant burned to the ground and long years of translation work went up in smoke.

Carey and his coworkers struggled against disease, poverty, natural disaster, political opposition, and the tragic death of Carey's wife and two of his children on the mission field. But they never gave up. His organization translated the Bible into thirty-four Asian languages, compiled dictionaries, founded a college, began countless churches and mission stations, started one hundred schools and many newspapers, and achieved tremendous social reform for the Indian people. If you were to travel in India today, you would find that his name still commands respect. The Spirit of God moved through the people of India as a result of Carey's work, and succeeding generations have trusted Christ as their Lord as a result.

Something else happened. Within a few years of William Carey's diligent efforts, the Western church was caught up in a Holy Spirit–directed world-missions movement. Evangelistic societies arose throughout the body of Christ. Think of it—God used one man, at great cost, to spark this mighty movement.

Now think about yourself. Once you have asked God to use you for His purposes, can you live in the firm, faithful expectancy that He will do so?

EXPECTING THE UNEXPECTED

I am confident that if we could speak with William Carey today, he would not show the least surprise that so many amazing accomplishments came to fruition because of the seed he had sown in the face of seemingly insurmountable odds. What else should Carey have expected from the sovereign, wise, and omnipotent God of this universe?

The Word of God tells us that "the eyes of the LORD search the whole earth in order to strengthen those whose hearts are fully committed to him" (2 Chronicles 16:9). In other words, our Lord is watching all the time, His eyes moving restlessly throughout the earth, sifting through this teeming planet to find a willing servant with a committed heart. Then, He acts to empower the servant to accomplish much.

Why do we not expect Him to honor His many promises to do mighty works through our hands?

He yearns to offer the wonderful gift of salvation, and He wishes to use us as His vessels to personally deliver that offer to every nation. The only limitation is found in the degree of our willingness to serve Him. So why should we be surprised when He acts powerfully and miraculously the first moment we make ourselves available? Why do we not expect Him to honor His many promises to do mighty works through our hands?

Perhaps it is ingrained in our human nature to expect as little from God as we expect from other people. We are all too often like the disciples. They followed along in the towns and villages as Jesus healed the sick from impossible illnesses, fed the hungry in impossible numbers, and even raised Lazarus from the impossible bed of death itself. Yet even given the presence of Jesus and His constant demonstrations and assurances of the power of God, again and again the disciples' faith faltered. Jesus rebuked His disciples for their lack of faith and pointed out that no miracles would occur for His followers as long as their hearts lacked supernatural expectation (Matthew 17:20).

On a visit to Nazareth, the hometown of Jesus, I shared a meal with one of the brightest and most successful men I knew in Israel. He supervised and promoted his country's tourism industry. We sat at a table in the local hotel, enjoying our lunch in the midst of a crowded room full of diners.

I had felt the prompting of the Holy Spirit to share my faith with this man, and I began to talk about the many great things Jesus Christ had done for me. I saw the flicker of interest in my new friend's eyes, so I looked forward to asking for His decision to receive Christ in some more solitary spot after lunch. But my friend did not want to wait! He wanted to pray while we were still at our table. And so, before a room full of his fellow Israelis, this successful businessman poured out a heartfelt prayer to God, asking the Lord to take over in his life.

As we concluded our lunch, my friend pleaded, "Dr. Bright, will you please send someone back to Nazareth to help me share this new truth with everyone I know?"

I immediately recognized the irony in his words: *new truth*. The good news of Christ is two thousand years old, and it emerged in—of all places in this world—that very city in which this man lived and worked. But for him it was a new discovery.

I thought of how Jesus had been treated when he visited His hometown of Nazareth at the beginning of His ministry. People He had known for years, even members of His family, could not believe that one of their own could possibly be the Son of God. "And so he did only a few miracles there because of their unbelief" (Matthew 13:58).

Where there is unbelief, no mountains will be moved, no sick people will be healed, no great works will be done for God's kingdom. Just as Jesus could do no mighty miracles in Nazareth because of the townspeople's unbelief, so today we limit His mighty miracles because of our unbelief.

His lesson to us is not to be distracted from His supernatural plans and acts in our lives by unbelieving, negative, and discouraging people.

On the other hand, Jesus consistently honored the faith of those who had the simple expectation that He would fulfill what He promised. One day, for example, a Roman centurion came to Him, concerned about an ailing servant. The official humbly urged Jesus not to enter the home, for he felt that his house was not worthy of having Jesus as a guest. Furthermore, the centurion felt Jesus did not have to be physically present under that roof to perform a miracle, because Jesus had power and authority over illness. As the centurion explained it: "Say the word, and my servant will be healed. For I myself am a man under authority, with soldiers under me. I tell this one, 'Go,' and he goes; and that one, 'Come,' and he comes. I say to my servant, 'Do this,' and he does it" (Luke 7:7–8 NIV).

> *Success is a matter of power and authority, and Jesus held the ultimate degrees of each.*

The Bible tells us Jesus found the centurion's faith to be remarkable, and He had seen none like it in Israel. It was simply a matter of the Roman official's having a firm grasp on the essential truth: Success is a matter of power and authority, and Jesus held the ultimate degrees of each.

To be a person of faith is to be a person who lives in a state of faithful expectancy that God will do what He has promised. He has the power; He has the authority; why would He not perform the great works He has carried out since the beginning of time?

We should be on the lookout all the time to see how God is moving in our life and the lives of others. We can then more easily cooperate with His work in the world and praise Him for the harvest He reaps. He will direct us all the way through a life of supernatural thinking and supernatural doing if we will only look for His movement and follow Him.

The disciple Thomas could not believe that Jesus' promise of resurrection would come true. After he felt the wounds and saw Jesus' resurrection was true, Jesus said, "You believe because you have seen me. Blessed are those who haven't seen me and believe anyway" (John 20:29).

We should be on the lookout all the time to see how God is moving in our life and the lives of others.

Most of us are like Thomas. For us, seeing is believing. But we must reverse that equation and learn that believing is seeing. If we truly wish to see the miracles that God wants to accomplish through us, we have to start believing that He will do them. He will not act through those who doubt.

The apostle James warned against the dangers of asking God for anything without really expecting Him to answer the prayer. The particular issue at hand was praying for wisdom, but the principle of faith in prayer relates to every kind of request we might make of God.

> If you need wisdom—if you want to know what God wants you to do—ask him, and he will gladly tell you. He will not resent your asking. But when you ask him, be sure that you really expect him to answer, for a doubtful mind is as unsettled as a wave of the sea that is driven and tossed by the wind. People like that should not expect to receive anything from the Lord. They can't make up their minds. They waver back and forth in everything they do.
>
> JAMES 1:5–8

Unbelief is a grave issue for those of us who claim to trust Christ as our Lord. What is the job of a believer but to believe? Doubting Thomases never make a great breakthrough; it is those who take Christ at His word who experience victories.

A MATTER OF FAITH

Pastor Bill Hybels and his staff, with a congregation then numbering just a few hundred, by faith raised money for and built a worship center seating thousands. It sat on a huge piece of property in the western suburbs of Chicago when the congregation first worshipped in it on February 15, 1981. Would such a large structure ever be filled with worshipers? Hybels and the other church leaders believed it would. And in fact, it was not long before the building was overflowing. Willow Creek Community Church has become one of the largest churches in the United States and a leader in reminding Christians that we are to reach out to nonbelievers.

The first week Wesley Stafford served as president of Compassion International, a child-development ministry, he was worshiping God alone in the prairies of Colorado. He was thinking about how his ministry might have one million sponsored children before his tenure as president was done when he heard God asking, "What about all the others?" Stafford then realized that even a million children represented just a drop in the bucket of all the needy children in the world. On that day in 1993, Stafford had to trust God that through a new initiative of child advocacy, his organization could help improve the lives of far more children than just those for whom they could find sponsors.

In the 1990s, Pastor Julio Ruibal dared to proclaim God in one of the most dangerous places on earth: Cali, Colombia.

Could God really change lives and the community in a place where the powerful and violent Colombian drug cartels ruled? Ruibal and others thought so. They began holding all-night prayer meetings once a month. These meetings had to be moved to a stadium when the numbers attending grew to the tens of thousands. Homicides in this murder-prone city dropped. Drug lords were arrested. Though Ruibal himself was eventually murdered, and though the situation remains difficult, thousands are still meeting Christ and being changed in Cali.

These supernatural thinkers and many others have had faith in God. They have expected great things to come from God, even though the situations they were in seemed risky or difficult. Of course, that is when a supernatural expectation matters the most—when things are not going smoothly.

PERSEVERING IN FAITH

Through our ministry with Campus Crusade for Christ International, we have often been put to the test. Many times we have waited for months, years, or even, on a few occasions, decades to see our prayers answered. As the Lord came through each time, providing an opportunity or a contribution that we desperately needed, our faith has grown stronger with each victory.

That is when a supernatural expectation matters the most—when things are not going smoothly.

During the 1970s, a vision from God began to take root within me. He impressed upon me to put together a university with global ambitions. I wanted to build an educational institution so magnificent that it would make an impact for the glory of God around the world. We wanted a Christian university that would attract people from every country—a Christian Harvard or Oxford. But we needed five thousand acres of land. We needed to build thousands of homes on a life estate concept to finance and ensure the future of the university.

The miracles continued to come. There were 5,043 acres available to us in one of the most beautiful regions of America. The officials were excited about the idea of the university, and they assured us that we could start building within eighteen months. But later, anti-Christian influences in the community opposed us, obstructing our development of the land. It was difficult to understand why a vision from God had come up against such a formidable wall, but after a quarter century of struggling, it was obvious the university would never be built on that land.

Then God, in His supernatural way, led me to a wonderful Christian who was the president of one of the largest U.S. community colleges. He was willing to serve our fledgling university as president, but he would not be available until his retirement five years later. We waited and continued to pray, but when he reached retirement age, his board of trustees would not release him. They insisted that he continue as president. Two years later he was honored as one of the leading educators in America.

Failing to get such a leader for our visionary educational enterprise seemed another obstacle for us, but God had plans we could not have anticipated. He showed me a man He had uniquely prepared to lead the university, J. Stanley Oakes. Today, he is doing a marvelous—and, I might add, *supernatural*—job as president of the King's College. In the meantime, the Internet has come of age. How could we, or anyone else, have foreseen its explosion?

The headquarters and complex for our educational initiative are now in the Empire State Building in New York, and our vision is no longer to train a few thousand international students on 5,000 acres at a cost of $200 million or more. Instead, our campus is the world. Our potential student enrollment is in the millions through Internet and satellite distribution. And the cost of leading such an endeavor is much less in the "virtual" world than it would be in the physical one.

Our original vision, impressive at the time, now seems puny next to what God has made possible for us. We followed His will in faith and trusted Him for the timing and the increase. Twenty-five years later, through His boundless and perfect wisdom, we are rejoicing over a much larger vision.

God is faithful and will always keep His promises. We can expect Him to do exceedingly abundantly above our greatest expectations. Though I cannot speak for you, I assure you that my expectations for His glory are very ambitious!

WALKING BY FAITH

In my more than eighty years, I have yet to see our Lord fail in His faithfulness. Nothing in the world is more certain or more trustworthy than the promises of God. Therefore, as you begin to live supernaturally, as you develop the mind of Christ, as you pray for desires that are His desires, as you begin to plan for the great day of reaping the harvest, and as you continue in His love, you must employ the principle of faithful expectancy.

A new day is here; what will God accomplish through you in it? On this new day, when He shows you a goal, thank Him in your heart. Praise our great God and Savior with every part of your being. Be joyful and go forth to live the day with a fresh idea of how His kingdom may be brought a little closer to our needy world through your devotion to Him and His work.

To be a supernatural thinker, you can and must walk by faith. Expect great things from God; attempt great things for God.

So far we have looked at supernatural thinking and the different actions required in supernatural thinking: supernatural trust, supernatural prayer, supernatural planning, supernatural love, and supernatural expectancy.

Now we come to the desired result of all this: supernatural victory.

10

Live It!

Since 1945, when I received Christ, I have experienced many miracles of God's grace from my Lord and Savior. Previously, my own human goals and aspirations had been small and temporary, but when I surrendered my life completely to God, His visions became mine—and His supernatural victory became accessible to me.

It seems like yesterday that God gave me the vision to begin a movement to help reach the world for Christ beginning with students. The rapid expansion of that movement to take in other campuses, countries, and continents was, in the minds of most of our friends, an impossible objective. However, God had given me a clear vision and the confidence that He would help me accomplish what He had called me to do. "God is working in you, giving you the desire to obey him and the power to do what pleases him" (Philippians 2:13).

I remember when our staff numbered less than fifty, and we celebrated the call of God to help fulfill the Great Commission. We placed a candle on our map of the world with as much confidence of seeing our goal reached as we have today with a full-time staff of nearly thirty thousand and over half a million trained volunteer staff. How? Our confidence was then, and is now, in the God who called us—not in our strength or ourselves.

It seems like yesterday that God began to nudge our ministry beyond the confines of the university campus, so that we were helping to evangelize the globe through innovative initiatives such as the EXPLO gatherings and the Here's Life world strategy. Impossible though it may have seemed, millions of people all across the world heard the gospel through unprecedented, Spirit-led movements of all kinds.

And it seems like a mere few days ago that we produced and began to show the *JESUS* film. What if you had suggested at the outset that we, or anyone else, could have shown a film of any kind—much less a film about Jesus—to more than six billion people in over eight hundred languages in approximately twenty years? Anyone might have said you had lost your mind!

Only the Holy Spirit could orchestrate such a mighty movement among so many people in so many corners of the world across so many barriers and obstacles and against every effort of the Prince of Darkness. Humanly speaking, it was impossible. But it was not impossible with God—everything is possible with Him. Best of all, there are still new worlds to conquer.

THE GREATEST JOY

The greatest joy in the world is to play a part in achieving supernatural goals for God. I am humbled and thankful to God that He has used someone as insignificant and unworthy as I to play a role in His fantastic plans for this world. There is no other life I would want to lead.

How about you? Are you ready to believe God for impossible goals? I have given a brief description of what my life has been like in that regard—what

The greatest joy in the world is to play a part in achieving supernatural goals for God.

would yours be like? You may feel insignificant or ordinary, but God has an important work for you to do.

Stop and try to imagine the kind of life I have been describing in this book. Assuming you are not already living supernaturally, can you envision what your life would look like and feel like if you began to let God live supernaturally through you? To let Him think His thoughts through your life—ideas that are far above and beyond the ordinary, projects with no room for mediocrity, visions of transcending excellence in touching and transforming the hearts and lives of all humanity?

The world is desperately in need of such an achiever. God is searching for such a person. As we have seen, His eyes move to and fro throughout the earth, looking for the one who is willing to step forward and say, "Here am I, Lord. Send me." If you have read this far, I trust and pray that you are such a person. I trust and pray that even now you can see yourself stepping forward from a throng as wide as humanity and saying, "Lord and Master, I trust You completely. I love You exclusively. I will follow You absolutely wherever You will lead me. Even if no one else follows, and even if no one else chooses to live the supernatural life, I will serve You as long as I live. Here am I—send me and empower me to achieve impossible, supernatural goals for Your eternal glory."

Indeed, if you decide to think with a supernatural mind-set and live the supernatural life, to trust God for the impossible, you will be a member of an exclusive group. Few people are

---------------❖---------------

You may feel insignificant or ordinary, but God has an important work for you to do.

----

willing to give themselves absolutely and wholeheartedly to the adventure of complete abandonment to God's will and leadership.

THE LANGUAGE OF HEAVEN

The longer I live, the more I see that we have spent more than enough time doing things in our mere human abilities. It is time for us to begin thinking and speaking the language of heaven—supernatural, superabundant thinking that confounds the world. God longs to see you and me live as He intended us to live, breaking down barriers and casting aside obstacles each day as we invite Him to achieve greater and greater wonders for Him.

The writer of Hebrews is referring to just such a life in this passage:

> Since we are surrounded by such a huge crowd of
> witnesses to the life of faith, let us strip off every weight
> that slows us down, especially the sin that so easily hinders
> our progress. And let us run with endurance the race that
> God has set before us. We do this by keeping our eyes on
> Jesus, on whom our faith depends from start to finish.
>
> 12:1–2

When you begin to run that race, you will indeed begin to strip off and throw away the hindrances that slow you down.

You will find yourself giving up lesser pursuits that once seemed important. You surely will find that you have less time for television, Web surfing, or other pastimes that no longer hold such attraction for you. The Spirit of God will be sifting your character, refining your desires, and drawing you onward toward the essence of your life—the reason why He put you on this earth. You will have had a taste of the supernatural life, of trusting God for the impossible. From now until God calls you home, no other lifestyle will hold any appeal for you.

As you begin to live with the supernatural mind-set God always intended you to have, your whole world will begin to change. The great change will begin with the way you see your surroundings. You will look at the world as God sees it. You will be thinking with the mind of Christ. The Holy Spirit will have such a firm hold on your life that you will be amazed to consider the thoughts you used to have, so greatly has your thinking changed.

All around you, as you see through the eyes of God, you will envision tasks He wants done. You will see needs that must be filled, goals that must be reached, and people who long to be loved and chaperoned into the presence of God. Not a single one of these tasks will seem a burden or a heavy responsibility, for the Spirit of God will fill you with joy and compassion, wisdom and strength, for the task.

Then, as you begin to take on the challenges that God shows you, He will lead others to gather around you. You will be amazed by the wonderful people whom God sends across your path, because the world is one great pasture filled with billions of sheep without a shepherd. The Lord will send mentors to teach you, students to learn from you, and caregivers to minister to your needs. You will be part of a dynamic and loving community of faith, through your church and through the many relationships God gives you. You will constantly be encouraging others, and you will constantly be encouraged.

Frequently, you will find yourself sharing your faith with nonbelievers. Like the apostle Paul, you will be able to say, "Everywhere we go, we tell everyone about Christ" (Colossians 1:28). And like Philip, who shared his faith with the Ethiopian (Acts 8), you will find that the Spirit of God will place you in strategic places at strategic times for people who are in crisis or who are being drawn to the love of God. You will smile each time you realize that God has maneuvered you into another setting of great opportunity. As you dynamically share your faith and introduce others to Christ, you will feel the joy of the most satisfying reward that life has to offer. Those whom you lead to Christ will likewise lead others to Him, and you will have the thrill of seeing new generations of God's children come into His kingdom.

You will find yourself serving more and more at the point of your gifts, for the Holy Spirit always works through the special spiritual gifts He has given us. As you do more for God, those gifts and skills will be sharpened. They will dovetail perfectly with the needs that loom in your path as you walk in the Spirit. You will discover new gifts you never knew you had.

Then you will see them—goals ahead of you that the world counts as impossible to achieve. They may not be of the type that attracts attention, but they are important for the kingdom in their own way. The Lord will place these high-impact goals on your mind and heart until they begin to burn within you. A great burden will develop until you know for certain that God wants you to take on these goals for Him. Perhaps He wants to send you to another part of the world. Perhaps He wants to send you to a brand-new work in life. Perhaps there is some new achievement that has never before been accomplished, and God has been saving it just for you.

You can be certain that there is such a grand vision for your life and that God has been preparing it for you since before you were born, as He spoke to Jeremiah: "I knew you before I formed you in your mother's womb. Before you were born I set you apart and appointed you as my spokesman to the world" (Jeremiah 1:5).

Jeremiah was no different from you or me. Just as God had a task for that prophet to accomplish, so He has a great task for you—or perhaps a whole series of them!

The Lord will place these high-impact goals on your mind and heart until they begin to burn within you.

I challenge you to embrace the work God has reserved for you. Feel the thrill of knowing there is at least one great victory that lies ahead for you, that the Lord placed it there with your name on it, and that in His strength all things are possible. Victory is certain.

SUPERNATURAL VICTORY

I challenge you to thank God today for the new life that lies ahead for you, a life of supernatural vision and high achievement. Praise His name for the people who are living in darkness, who are bound to see a great light because God will use you to lead them to it. Believe me, you cannot even begin to imagine the wonders that lie in store for you as you make yourself available for His use.

A great journey begins with a single step, and you can

begin to know the joy of serving God the second you ask Him to inspire you with supernatural thinking. Until we meet again in the great throng surrounding the throne of the King, when you can share your joy with me in the telling of your story, I send you onward with a prayer of my most sincere and heart-felt encouragement, to a life of supreme supernatural victory dedicated to the eternal glory of our great Creator God and Savior.

Readers' Guide

For Personal Reflection or Group Discussion

Questions are an inevitable part of life. Proud parents ask their new baby, "Can you smile?" Later they ask, "Can you say 'Mama'?" "Can you walk to Daddy?" The early school years bring the inevitable, "What did you learn at school today?" Later school years introduce tougher questions, "If X equals 12 and Y equals –14, then …?" Adulthood adds a whole new set of questions. "Should I remain single or marry?" "How did things go at the office?" "Did you get a raise?" "Should we let Susie start dating?" "Which college is right for Kyle?" "How can we possibly afford to send our kids to college?"

This book raises questions too. The following study guide is designed to (1) maximize the subject material and (2) apply biblical truth to daily life. You won't be asked to solve any algebraic problems or recall dates associated with obscure events in history, so relax. Questions asking for objective information are based solely on the text. Most questions, however, prompt you to search inside your soul, examine the circumstances that surround your life, and decide how you can best use the truths communicated in the book.

Honest answers to real issues can strengthen your faith, draw you closer to the Lord, and lead you into fuller, richer, more joyful, and productive daily adventures. So confront each question head-on and expect the One who is the answer for all of life's questions and needs to accomplish great things in your life.

CHAPTER 1: THE GREATEST ADVENTURE OF YOUR LIFE

1. How does the author define *supernatural thinking*?

2. Dr. Bright based his ministry on "God is working in you, giving you the desire to obey Him and the power to do what pleases Him" (Philippians 2:13). Give an example of a time when God empowered you to complete a task.

CHAPTER 2: THE CASE FOR DIFFERENT THINKING

1. What sets "world Christians" apart from other Christians?

2. What characteristics of supernatural thinking do you believe are most lacking today? Defend your answer.

3. Do you know any Christians who are supernatural Christians? Why do you consider them supernatural thinkers?

4. What do you think you need to do to become a supernatural thinker?

5. How might your life change if you think supernaturally?

CHAPTER 3: THINKING THAT GOES ABOVE AND BEYOND

1. How do you differentiate between positive thinking and supernatural thinking?

2. How did supernatural thinking make a positive impact on South Korea in the early 1970s? How might it make an impact on your community today?

3. How might a transformed mind cause Christians to rearrange their priorities?

4. What role does God assume in transforming the believer's mind? What role does the believer assume in this process?

5. What emotional changes might you experience as your mind becomes transformed?

CHAPTER 4: THE PROCESS OF SUPERNATURAL THINKING

1. Why is it impossible for an nonbeliever to think supernaturally?

2. How did your thinking change when you became a believer? To what do you credit this change?

3. How does the author explain what he calls "Spiritual Breathing"? Why is this practice necessary if a believer wants to think supernaturally?

4. What vision do you believe Christians collectively need today? What vision has God given you?

5. What obstacles will you trust God to overcome in your life as you serve Him?

CHAPTER 5: TRUSTING GOD SUPERNATURALLY

1. How do you explain the fact that some Christians appear to lead lives that are no different from those of nonbelievers?

2. How do you define "carnal life"?

3. What four prerequisites to being filled with the Spirit does the author cite?

4. What positive changes does the filling of the Spirit make in a Christian's life?

5. How effective is a believer's witness to his or her unbelieving friends and family members without the filling with the Spirit? What would nonbelievers see most prominently in the life of a believer who is filled with the Spirit?

CHAPTER 6: PRAYING SUPERNATURALLY

1. How is supernatural thinking related to our firsthand knowledge of God?

2. Why must supernatural thinking precede supernatural praying?

3. What impresses you most about Jesus' prayers?

4. How can Christians keep their prayers focused on God's will?

5. What steps will you take to pray supernaturally?

CHAPTER 7: PLANNING SUPERNATURALLY

1. How can making plans be a supernatural process?

2. What guidelines for supernatural planning does the author recommend? Why do you think they are important?

3. What spiritual goals should every Christian plan to reach?

4. How does knowing God's Word help the believer to plan wisely?

5. Do you agree that faith and financial planning are mutually exclusive? Why or why not?

CHAPTER 8: LOVING SUPERNATURALLY

1. Can a believer despise his or her enemies while possessing supernatural love? Why or why not?

2. What part of the story of Dr. Kim grips you most powerfully? Why?

3. How does a believer acquire *agape* love?

4. How are love and faith related?

5. Who is waiting to receive unconditional love from you?

CHAPTER 9: EXPECTING SUPERNATURAL RESULTS

1. Why is it not presumptuous to expect supernatural results when we serve God?

2. What results did people receive by faith in Jesus during His ministry on earth? Why did Christian service described in the book of Acts enjoy supernatural results?

3. Do you agree that doubt is pervasive among twenty-first-century Christians? Defend your answer.

4. What supernatural results should you and your fellow believers anticipate by faith?

5. How might expecting supernatural results affect your attitude at work, at home, and at church?

CHAPTER 10: LIVE IT!

1. What victories should every Christian anticipate?

2. What hindrances generally slow most Christians as they run the race of life?

3. How will God help believers who accept the challenges He gives them?

4. How might the believer's allotment of time shift as he or she accepts the new challenges God gives?

5. What encourages you most to take on new ventures for God?

Appendix A

Your PACT with God

You could read this book repeatedly and memorize every line, but if it does not translate into a change in the way you live, your time will have been spent in vain. If you do desire to live the powerful, visionary, Spirit-filled, and Spirit-directed life we have explored together in these pages, it would be appropriate to finish this book with a pact between you and your loving Lord and Master. And as you begin your new life, I would like to leave you with a simple, four-word summary that encapsulates the idea of thinking supernaturally. I am indebted to my son Brad for helping me find just the right four memorable words. Together they create the acrostic "PACT":

P RAYER

Pray without ceasing. Confess your sins the moment you even start to consider them. Let the mind of Christ guide you in thinking and planning.

ATTRIBUTES OF GOD

If you meditate daily on God's wonderful attributes, you will experience His holiness constantly. You will live supernaturally.

CONFLICT

Expect and prepare for spiritual conflict. Wear the whole armor of God (Ephesians 6:10–18). Resist the Devil, and remember that God's power is infinitely superior.

TELLING

Keep telling everyone you know about Jesus. The best way I know to maintain a supernatural perspective is to take part in the greatest supernatural activity known to humankind, the bringing of a sinner to salvation and forgiveness in Christ.

Will you make this PACT with God today? Let the words on the next page be a guide to your prayer as you and your Lord establish a covenant to be followed and honored until the dawn of eternity.

Precious Lord,

I come before You to make a solemn and yet joyful covenant. I realize now, better than ever, just how wide and how deep and how powerful is Your love for me. I can never deserve it, nor even come close, but only accept Your gracious gift with a grateful heart. I realize now that You never intended that I live a life of quiet, passionless mediocrity. And I can never go back to the small plans and uninspiring goals of my past. I want to pursue impossible goals and supernatural achievements for Your honor and glory. My pact is to be Your instrument in every way, in every direction You will use me, during every moment of every day for the rest of my life. My pact is to commit myself wholeheartedly to Your wonderful, loving, and supernatural will. My pact is to be Your hands, feet, and voice for the fulfilling of the Great Commission year after year in my lifetime. In other words, I make this pact for the greatest adventure life has to offer, for the greatest goal set before us—the goal of laying every earthly crown and supernatural achievement at Your feet on that day when I will kneel humbly before Your throne. Until then, O Lord, I am Yours and only Yours—for supernatural thinking, for supernatural living, and for supernatural accomplishment—from this moment until the dawn of eternity itself. This is my solemn, sincere, and joyful covenant.

Name   Steve Smit

Date   March 9, 2007

Appendix B

God's Word on Supernatural Thinking

Following are selected Scripture references that were presented throughout the text of this book. We encourage you to sit down with your Bible and review these verses in their context, prayerfully reflecting upon what God's Word tells you about the joy of supernatural thinking.

CHAPTER 1

Mark 10:27

Mark 9:23

Philippians 4:13

CHAPTER 2

John 14:12, 14

Proverbs 23:7

1 Corinthians 2:16

Romans 12:2

Matthew 28:18–20

Hebrews 11:6

Acts 1:8

Zechariah 4:6

John 15:21

Philippians 3:13–14

Joshua 1:8

Exodus 20:8

1 Corinthians 10:13

CHAPTER 3

Luke 18:27

Ephesians 3:20

Isaiah 55:8–9

2 Corinthians 3:18

1 Peter 4:1

CHAPTER 4

Philippians 3:8

Ephesians 5:18

1 John 1:9

Isaiah 43:19

1 Corinthians 12

Matthew 25:21

Judges 7
Matthew 18:4
James 4:6
Matthew 20:25–28
Philippians 1:6
Numbers 13:30
Numbers
   13:32–33
2 Corinthians 5:7

CHAPTER 5

Genesis 3
Isaiah 53:6
1 Corinthians 2:14
1 Corinthians
   3:1–3
John 15:5
Romans 8:9
John 7:37–38
Colossians 2:13–14

1 John 5:14–15

CHAPTER 6

Matthew 21:21–22
2 Timothy 1:12
Mark 1:35
Matthew 6:9–13
Matthew 26:39
Jeremiah 33:3

CHAPTER 7

2 Timothy 1:7
Proverbs 16:3
Proverbs 16:1
James 1:5
Proverbs 16:9
Luke 14:28–30
Matthew 25:14–30

CHAPTER 8

1 Corinthians
   13:4–7
Romans 8:38–39
Matthew 22:37–40
1 John 4:9–11
Romans 5:5
Romans 8:7–8
Philippians 2

CHAPTER 9

2 Chronicles 16:9
Matthew 17:20
Matthew 13:58
Luke 7:7–8
John 20:29

CHAPTER 10

Hebrews 12:1–2
Colossians 1:28
Jeremiah 1:5

About the Author

DR. BILL BRIGHT, fueled by his passion to share the love and claims of Jesus Christ with "every living person on earth," was the founder and president of Campus Crusade for Christ. The world's largest Christian ministry, Campus Crusade serves people in 191 countries through a staff of 26,000 full-time employees and more than 225,000 trained volunteers working in some sixty targeted ministries and projects that range from military ministry to inner-city ministry.

Bill Bright was so motivated by what is known as the Great Commission, Christ's command to carry the gospel throughout the world, that in 1956 he wrote a booklet titled *The Four Spiritual Laws*, which has been printed in 200 languages and distributed to more than 2.5 billion people. Other books Bright authored include *Discover the Book God Wrote, God: Discover His Character, Come Help Change Our World, The Holy Spirit: The Key to Supernatural Living, Life Without Equal, Witnessing Without Fear, Coming Revival, Journey Home,* and *Red Sky in the Morning.*

In 1979 Bright commissioned the *JESUS* film, a feature-length dramatization of the life of Christ. To date, the film has been viewed by more than 5.7 billion people in 191 countries and has become the most widely viewed and translated film in history.

Dr. Bright died in July 2003 before the final editing of this book. But he prayed that it would leave a legacy of his love for Jesus and the power of the Holy Spirit to change lives. He is survived by his wife, Vonette; their sons and daughters-in-law; and four grandchildren.

THE LIFETIME TEACHINGS OF

Written by one of Christianity's most respected and beloved teachers, this series is a must for every believer's library. Each of the books in the series focuses on a vital aspect of a meaningful life of faith: trusting God, accepting Christ, living a spirit-filled life, intimacy with God, forgiveness, prayer, obedience, supernatural thinking, giving, and sharing Christ with others.

Dr. Bill Bright was the founder of Campus Crusade for Christ Intl., the world's largest Christian ministry. He commissioned the JESUS film, a documentary on the life of Christ that has been translated into more than 800 languages.

EACH BOOK INCLUDES A CELEBRITY-READ ABRIDGED AUDIO CD!

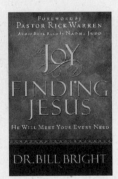

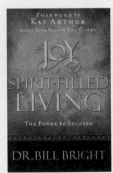

Joy of Trusting God
Foreword by Billy Graham
Audio by John Tesh
0-78144-246-X

Joy of Finding Jesus
Foreword by Pastor
Rick Warren
Audio by Naomi Judd
0-78144-247-8

Joy of Spirit-Filled Living
Foreword by Kay Arthur
Audio by Ricky Skaggs
0-78144-248-6

DR. BILL BRIGHT

FOUNDER OF CAMPUS CRUSADE FOR CHRIST

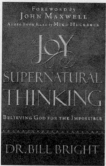

Joy of Supernatural Thinking
Foreword by John Maxwell
Audio by Gov. Mike Huckabee
0-78144-253-2

Joy of Dynamic Giving
Foreword by Charles Stanley
Audio by John Schneider
0-78144-254-0

Joy of Sharing Jesus
Foreword by Pat Robertson
Audio by Kathie Lee Gifford
0-78144-255-9

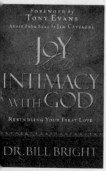

Joy of Intimacy with God
Foreword by Tony Evans
Audio by Amy Grant
0-78144-249-4

Joy of Total Forgiveness
Foreword by Gary Smalley
Audio by Janine Turner
0-78144-250-8

Joy of Active Prayer
Foreword by Max Lucado
Audio by Joni Earekcson Tada
0-78144-251-6

Joy of Faithful Obedience
Foreword by Tim LaHaye
Audio by Kirk Franklin
0-78144-252-4

Collect all 10 of These Foundational Works!

The Word at Work Around the World

A vital part of Cook Communications Ministries is our international outreach, Cook Communications Ministries International (CCMI). Your purchase of s book, and of other books and Christian-growth products from Cook, enables MI to provide Bibles and Christian literature to people in more than 150 guages in 65 countries.

Cook Communications Ministries is a not-for-profit, self-supporting organiza- n. Revenues from sales of our books, Bible curricula, and other church and home oducts not only fund our U.S. ministry, but also fund our CCMI ministry around the rld. One hundred percent of donations to CCMI go to our international literature grams.

MI reaches out internationally in three ways:

ur premier International Christian Publishing Institute (ICPI) trains leaders om nationally led publishing houses around the world.

e provide literature for pastors, evangelists, and Christian workers in their ational language.

e reach people at risk—refugees, AIDS victims, street children, and famine ictims—with God's Word.

ord Power, God's Power

th Kidz, RiverOak, Honor, Life Journey, Victor, NexGen — every time you purchase ook produced by Cook Communications Ministries, you not only meet a vital rsonal need in your life or in the life of someone you love, but you're also a part of nistering to José in Colombia, Humberto in Chile, Gousa in India, or Lidiane in azil. You help make it possible for a pastor in China, a child in Peru, or a mother in st Africa to enjoy a life-changing book. And because you helped, children and ilts around the world are learning God's Word and walking in his ways.

Thank you for your partnership in helping to disciple the world. May God bless with the power of his Word in your life.

r more information about our ternational ministries, visit www.ccmi.org.

Additional copies of
THE JOY OF SUPERNATURAL THINKING
and other titles in "The Joy of Knowing God" series
are available wherever good books are sold.

✠ ✠ ✠

If you have enjoyed this book,
or if it has had an impact on your life,
we would like to hear from you.

Please contact us at:

VICTOR BOOKS
Cook Communications Ministries, Dept. 201
4050 Lee Vance View
Colorado Springs, CO 80918

Or at our Web site: www.cookministries.com

Victor®
The Bible Teacher's Teacher